Collins

AQA
Step up to English

Teacher Resource Pack

Tom Spindler, Sharon Stark
and David Hiam

William Collins' dream of knowledge for all began with the publication of his first book in 1819.

A self-educated mill worker, he not only enriched millions of lives, but also founded a flourishing publishing house. Today, staying true to this spirit, Collins books are packed with inspiration, innovation and practical expertise. They place you at the centre of a world of possibility and give you exactly what you need to explore it.

Collins. Freedom to teach
HarperCollins*Publishers*
The News Building
1 London Bridge Street
London SE1 9GF

HarperCollins*Publishers*, 1st Floor, Watermarque Building, Ringsend Road, Dublin 4, Ireland

Browse the complete Collins catalogue at
www.collins.co.uk

> This textbook has been approved by AQA for use with our qualification. This means that we have checked that it broadly covers the specification and we are satisfied with the overall quality. Full details of our approval process can be found on our website.
>
> We approve textbooks because we know how important it is for teachers and students to have the right resources to support their teaching and learning. However, the publisher is ultimately responsible for the editorial control and quality of this book.
>
> Please note that when teaching the AQA Step Up to English (5970) course, you must refer to AQA's specification as your definitive source of information. While this book has been written to match the specification, it cannot provide complete coverage of every aspect of the course.
>
> A wide range of other useful resources can be found on the relevant subject pages of our website: aqa.org.uk

© HarperCollins*Publishers* 2016

10 9 8 7 6

ISBN 978-0-00-815218-5

Collins® is a registered trademark of HarperCollins*Publishers* Limited

A catalogue record for this book is available from the British Library

Tom Spindler, Sharon Stark and David Hiam assert their moral rights to be identified as the authors of this work.

With thanks to Mike Gould and Sabrina Sulliman.

Commissioning Editor: Catherine Martin and Ben Pettitt
Editor: Sue Chapple
Copy-editor: Hugh Hillyard-Parker
Project manager: Alexander Rutherford
Proof-reader: Rosamund Connelly
Cover designer: ink-tank and associates
Production controller: Rachel Weaver
Typesetter: Hugh Hillyard-Parker
Illustrations: QBS
Cover images © Dudarev Mikhail/Shutterstock, balabolka/Shutterstock

All rights reserved. No part of this book may be reproduced, stored in a retrieval system, or transmitted in any form or by any means, electronic, mechanical, photocopying, recording or otherwise, without the prior permission in writing of the Publisher. This book is sold subject to the conditions that it shall not, by way of trade or otherwise, be lent, re-sold, hired out or otherwise circulated without the Publisher's prior consent in any form of binding or cover other than that in which it is published and without a similar condition including this condition being imposed on the subsequent purchaser.

HarperCollins does not warrant that www.collins.co.uk or any other website mentioned in this title will be provided uninterrupted, that any website will be error free, that defects will be corrected, or that the website or the server that makes it available are free of viruses or bugs. For full terms and conditions please refer to the site terms provided on the website.

Contents

Introduction 4

Medium-term plans 6

Component 1 Lesson plans
Literacy topics

Topic 1 Celebrities
1 'I want to be famous' 16
2 What is it like to be a celebrity? 18
3 Celebrities in the 19th century 20
4 Do some people deserve to be famous? 22
5 What would you like to be famous for? 24
6 Should we ever feel sorry for celebrities? 26

Topic 2 Detectives
1 The skills of a good detective 28
2 Could you be a detective? 30
3 Crime in the 19th century 32
4 Do detectives just investigate crimes? 34
5 What makes detectives exciting? 36
6 Do you have good detective skills? 38

Topic 3 Exhibitions
1 What is an exhibition? 40
2 The Ideal Home Show 42
3 The history of exhibitions 44
4 Famous museums 46
5 An exhibition near you 48
6 Planning an exhibition 50

Topic 4 Travel
1 Where to go on holiday? 52
2 What would you tell people about your holiday? 54
3 Holidays in the 19th century 56
4 Exciting holiday destinations 58
5 Holidays of the future 60
6 What can go wrong on holiday? 62

Topic 5 Volunteering
1 Lending a hand 64
2 Wanted – volunteers of all ages 66
3 People, animals and events 68
4 Recruiting volunteers 70
5 The benefits of volunteering 72
6 Valuable volunteers 74

Component 2 Lesson plans
Creative writing and reading

Topic 1 Adventure
1 Race to the Pole 76
2 Why the Norwegians won the race 78
3 A passion for climbing 80
4 In search of adventure 82
5 Survival 84
6 A big adventure 86

Topic 2 Education
1 What makes a good teacher? 88
2 What makes a good student? 90
3 Learning in the 19th century 92
4 School holidays 94
5 A different point of view 96
6 Invitation to a school event 98

Topic 3 Fashion
1 What is fashion? 100
2 Work wear 102
3 What's the difference? 104
4 Following fashion 106
5 Fashion in the 19th century 108
6 Getting ready for a party 110

Topic 4 Sport
1 Supporting a team or person 112
2 Rival supporters 114
3 Making a match sound exciting 116
4 The supporter's view 118
5 The perfect player 120
6 How to be a sports writer 122

Topic 5 Transport
1 Full steam ahead 124
2 A traveller's diary 126
3 The long cycle ride 128
4 Flying high 130
5 Travelling to France 132
6 Cars in the future 134

Appendices
Spoken language support frames 136
Self-assessment sheets 140

© HarperCollins*Publishers* 2016

Introduction

The Collins *AQA Step up to English Teacher Resource Pack* is designed to support you in delivering AQA's Step up to English qualification, whether you are teaching students in a mixed-ability or an ability-banded context, and whether your students are working towards starting GCSE or securing an entry-level qualification.

In order to engage your learners, we have endeavoured to include a wide range of tasks and scenarios for students to respond to. Learners will have the chance to become a detective, manage a football team and advertise a holiday in space. Students will be asked to hold discussions, hot-seat each other and write a variety of different texts. All the while, they will be learning the foundational skills that will lead, where appropriate, towards success in the AQA GCSE course.

Using the Resource Pack

Each topic in the AQA specification is covered by six lessons. These two-page lesson plans have been included in the printed pack. Word and PDF versions of the lesson plans, as well as a wealth of supporting worksheets (differentiated for Entry Level 1, Entry Level 2 and Entry Level 3 learners), a PowerPoint presentation to help you deliver each lesson, and a GCSE-ready extension task for each topic are available to download here:
collins.co.uk/AQAstepuptoEnglish/download

Planning

The **medium-term plans** provide an overview of learning and the Assessment Objective coverage in each topic, to aid your planning.

Each lesson has as its focus one **Assessment Objective**, listed in bold at the start of the lesson plan. The **differentiated learning outcomes** make clear which thread of the AO is being addressed and what will be expected from students at each level.

Engagement

Video links and images on the **PowerPoints** offer a visual way into each topic, to get students engaged at the start of the lesson.

Topics have been chosen to excite and intrigue teenage students and **texts** have been tailored precisely to their reading and interest ages.

Several lessons feature extracts from fiction and non-fiction titles in the Collins *Read On* series (www.collins.co.uk/readon). You may like to explore these titles in full alongside your teaching of the relevant topics.

Supporting skills development

Familiar features from our AQA-approved GCSE English Language and English Literature resources have been used to support those students who will be making the transition to GCSE.

The **Big question** starter and **Big answer plenary** direct and draw together students' learning about the topic in each lesson. Students are guided through a clear learning sequence from **Getting you thinking**, **Explore the skills** and **Develop the skills**, where skills are introduced, modelled and practised, to a final task in **Apply the skills** where they have the chance to apply what they have learnt.

Differentiated **Spoken language support frames** have been included in an **appendix** at the end of the Resource Pack to help students understand what will make them successful when they are giving or listening to a presentation, asking or responding to questions, and taking part in a group discussion.

Differentiation

For every lesson two to three **differentiated worksheets** have been included at three levels (EL1, EL2 and EL3) to enable you to teach a mixed-ability class, should you wish, or to choose the resources most appropriate to your students' current level, to help them gain confidence and make progress. These tailored activities will allow students to work on the same piece of work, at the level that is appropriate to them.

A **GCSE-ready extension task** for each topic has been included to provide the bridging skills some students will need to progress to GCSE.

Assessment for learning

Self-assessment sheets are provided in different formats for Entry Level 1, Entry Level 2 and Entry Level 3 learners to help you and individual learners assess their progress in each topic. We would recommend that these are filled out at the start of the lesson – to focus students on the skills to be covered – and at the end of the lesson to review progress and set goals for future sessions.

With the greater challenge of new GCSE specifications, we believe that it is increasingly demanding for teachers to support students at all stages of their development. This challenge is further heightened by the reality that the majority of classes will contain students with a wide range of needs and capabilities. We have designed this resource pack to assist you to meet these challenges and to engage all students with a creative and exploratory approach to studying English. We hope it will provide an invaluable tool to help you support your students in taking their next steps in English.

Tom Spindler and Sharon Stark

Component 1   Medium-term plans

Topic 1 Celebrities

Lesson	Assessment Objectives	Big question
1 'I want to be famous'	**AO1** Read and understand a range of texts: Identify and interpret explicit and implicit information and ideas. AO7 AO8	How does someone become famous?
2 What is it like to be a celebrity?	**AO5** Communicate clearly, effectively and imaginatively, selecting and adapting tone, style and register for different forms, purposes and audiences.	What is a day in the life of a celebrity like?
3 Celebrities in the 19th century	**AO1** Read and understand a range of texts: Identify and interpret explicit and implicit information and ideas. AO9	What kind of celebrities were there in the 19th century?
4 Do some people deserve to be famous?	**AO4** Evaluate texts and support this with appropriate textual references. AO8	Do some people deserve to be famous?
5 What would you like to be famous for?	**AO5** Organise information and ideas, using structural and grammatical features to support coherence and cohesion of texts.	If you were a celebrity, what would you be famous for?
6 Should we ever feel sorry for celebrities?	**AO6** Use vocabulary and sentence structures for clarity, purpose and effect, with accurate spelling and punctuation. AO7 AO9	Should we ever feel sorry for celebrities?

GCSE-ready extension tasks	Assessment Objectives	NEA question types	How it helps prepare for GCSE
Reading a newspaper article Group discussion Individual presentation	**AO7** Demonstrate presentation skills. **AO8** Listen and respond appropriately to spoken language, including to questions and feedback on presentations. **AO9** Use spoken English effectively in speeches and presentations.	Builds skills for Component 1 Spoken language assessment	Builds skills for the GCSE English Language Spoken language NEA

Topic 2 Detectives

Lesson	Assessment Objectives	Big question	
1 The skills of a good detective	**AO1** Read and understand a range of texts: identify and interpret explicit and implicit information and ideas. AO7 AO9	What skills do you need to be a detective?	
2 Could you be a detective?	**AO5** Communicate clearly, effectively and imaginatively, selecting and adapting tone, style and register for different forms, purposes and audiences.	Could you be a detective?	
3 Crime in the 19th century	**AO1** Read and understand a range of texts: identify and interpret explicit and implicit information and ideas. AO8	What kind of crimes did detectives have to solve in the 19th century?	
4 Do detectives just investigate crimes?	**AO4** Evaluate texts and support this with appropriate textual references.	Do detectives just investigate crimes?	
5 What makes detectives exciting?	**AO5** Organise information and ideas, using structural and grammatical features to support coherence and cohesion of texts.	What makes detectives exciting?	
6 Do you have good detective skills?	**AO6** Use vocabulary and sentence structures for clarity, purpose and effect, with accurate spelling and punctuation. AO7 AO9	Do you have good detective skills?	
GCSE-ready extension tasks	**Assessment Objectives**	**NEA question types**	**How it helps prepare for GCSE**
Producing a leaflet	**AO5** Organise information and ideas, using structural and grammatical features to support coherence and cohesion of texts. **AO6** Use vocabulary and sentence structures for clarity, purpose and effect, with accurate spelling and punctuation.	Builds skills for Component 1 Writing task	Builds skills in producing texts for different audiences and purposes

Topic 3 Exhibitions

Lesson	Assessment Objectives	Big question	
1 What is an exhibition?	**AO1** Read and understand a range of texts: identify and interpret explicit and implicit information and ideas. **AO9**	What is an exhibition?	
2 The Ideal Home Show	**AO1** Read and understand a range of texts: identify and interpret explicit and implicit information and ideas.	What is the Ideal Home Show?	
3 The history of exhibitions	**AO1** Read and understand a range of texts: identify and interpret explicit and implicit information and ideas.	Why do we go to exhibitions?	
4 Famous museums	**AO5** **AO6** Use vocabulary and sentence structures for clarity, purpose and effect, with accurate spelling and punctuation.	What are museums?	
5 An exhibition near you	**AO5** **AO6** Use vocabulary and sentence structures for clarity, purpose and effect, with accurate spelling and punctuation.	What type of exhibitions are there in your area?	
6 Planning an exhibition	**AO5** **AO8** Listen and respond appropriately to spoken language, including to questions and feedback on presentations.	How do you plan an exhibition?	
GCSE-ready extension tasks	**Assessment Objectives**	**NEA question types**	**How it helps prepare for GCSE**
Reading an opinion piece Analysing viewpoint and the language used to communicate point of view Writing own point-of-view piece	**AO4** Evaluate texts and support this with appropriate textual references. **AO5** Communicate clearly, effectively and imaginatively, selecting and adapting tone, style and register for different forms, purposes and audiences. **AO6:** Use vocabulary and sentence structures for clarity, purpose and effect, with accurate spelling and punctuation.	Builds skills for Component 1 Reading and Writing tasks	Builds skills for the reading and writing tasks on GCSE English Language Paper 2 Writer's viewpoints and perspectives

Topic 4 Travel

Lesson	Assessment Objectives	Big question
1 Where to go on holiday?	**AO1** Read and understand a range of texts: Identify and interpret explicit and implicit information and ideas.	How do people choose where to go on holiday?
2 What would you tell people about your holiday?	AO1 **AO5** Communicate clearly, effectively and imaginatively, selecting and adapting tone, style and register for different forms, purposes and audiences.	What would you tell people about your holiday?
3 Holidays in the 19th century	**AO1** Read and understand a range of texts: Identify and interpret explicit and implicit information and ideas. AO8	Where did people go on holiday in the 19th century?
4 Exciting holiday destinations	**AO7** Demonstrate presentation skills. AO9	How do you make a holiday destination sound exciting?
5 Holidays of the future	**AO8** Listen and respond appropriately to spoken language, including to questions and feedback on presentations.	Where will people go on holiday in the future?
6 What can go wrong on holiday?	**AO6** Use vocabulary and sentence structures for clarity, purpose and effect, with accurate spelling and punctuation.	What can go wrong on holiday?

GCSE-ready extension tasks	Assessment Objectives	NEA question types	How it helps prepare for GCSE
Reading a piece of C18th century travel writing Comprehension and language analysis tasks	**AO2** Explain and comment on how writers use language and structure to achieve effects and influence readers, using relevant subject terminology to support views. **AO3** Compare writers' ideas and perspectives.	Builds skills for Component 1 Reading tasks	Builds skills for the reading tasks on GCSE English Language Paper 2 Writer's viewpoints and perspectives

Topic 5 Volunteering

Lesson	Assessment Objectives	Big question	
1 Lending a hand	AO1 Read and understand a range of texts: Identify and interpret explicit and implicit information and ideas. AO2	What is volunteering?	
2 Wanted – volunteers of all ages	AO5 AO6 Use vocabulary and sentence structures for clarity, purpose and effect, with accurate spelling and punctuation	How can you volunteer?	
3 People, animals and events	AO1 Read and understand a range of texts: Identify and interpret explicit and implicit information and ideas.	What types of opportunities are there for volunteering?	
4 Recruiting volunteers	AO5 Communicate clearly, effectively and imaginatively, selecting and adapting tone, style and register for different forms, purposes and audiences.	How can I find volunteers?	
5 The benefits of volunteering	AO1 Read and understand a range of texts: Identify and interpret explicit and implicit information and ideas. AO4	What are the benefits of volunteering?	
6 Valuable volunteers	AO7 AO8 Listen and respond appropriately to spoken language, including to questions and feedback on presentations AO9	What makes a good volunteer?	
GCSE-ready extension tasks	**Assessment Objectives**	**NEA question types**	**How it helps prepare for GCSE**
Group debate Individual presentation	AO8 Listen and respond appropriately to spoken language, including to questions and feedback on presentations	Builds skills for the Component 1 Spoken language task	Builds skills for the GCSE English Language Spoken language NEA

Component 2 Medium-term plans

Topic 1 Adventure

Lesson	Assessment Objectives	Big question
1 Race to the Pole	AO1 Read and understand a range of texts: Identify and interpret explicit and implicit information and ideas. AO7 AO8	Who won the race to the South Pole?
2 Why the Norwegians won the race	AO3 Compare writers' ideas and perspectives.	Why did the Norwegians win the race?
3 A passion for climbing	AO2 Explain and comment on how writers use language and structure to achieve effects and influence readers, using relevant subject terminology to support views. AO6	Would you risk losing your life?
4 In search of adventure	AO1 Read and understand a range of texts: Identify and interpret explicit and implicit information and ideas.	How can you find adventure?
5 Survival	AO5 AO6 Use vocabulary and sentence structures for clarity, purpose and effect with accurate spelling and punctuation.	What do you need to survive?
6 A big adventure	AO5 AO6 Use vocabulary and sentence structures for clarity, purpose and effect with accurate spelling and punctuation.	What would your big adventure be?

GCSE-ready extension tasks	Assessment Objectives	NEA question types	How it helps prepare for GCSE
Write a description	AO1 Read and understand a range of texts: Identify and interpret explicit and implicit information and ideas. AO6 Use vocabulary and sentence structures for clarity, purpose and effect with accurate spelling and punctuation.	Builds skills for Component 2 NEA Questions 1, 2 and 4 Builds skills for Component 2 NEA writing tasks Questions 8 and 9	Builds skills for GCSE English Language Paper 1 Question 5 (Descriptive writing)

Topic 2 Education

Lesson	Assessment Objectives	Big question
1 What makes a good teacher?	AO1 Read and understand a range of texts: identify and interpret explicit and implicit information and ideas.	What makes a good teacher?
2 What makes a good student?	AO2 AO5 AO6 Use vocabulary and sentence structures for clarity, purpose and effect, with accurate spelling and punctuation.	What makes a good student?
3 Learning in the 19th century	AO1 Read and understand a range of texts: identify and interpret explicit and implicit information and ideas.	How cool would it be not to have to go to school?
4 School holidays	AO5 AO6 Use vocabulary and sentence structures for clarity, purpose and effect with accurate spelling and punctuation.	Are school holidays too long?
5 A different point of view	AO3 Compare writers' ideas and perspectives.	How can you pick out the similarities and differences in a text?
6 Invitation to a school event	AO5 Communicate clearly, effectively and imaginatively, selecting and adapting tone, style and register for different forms, purposes and audiences. AO6	When did you last write a letter?

GCSE-ready extension tasks	Assessment Objectives	NEA question types	How it helps prepare for GCSE
Read a narrative passage based on a nineteenth-century novel (*Jane Eyre*) and comment on the writer's language choices. Plan and write a story.	AO2 Explain and comment on how writers use language and structure to achieve effects and influence readers, using relevant subject terminology to support views. AO5 Communicate clearly, effectively and imaginatively, selecting and adapting tone, style and register for different forms, purposes and audiences. AO6 Use vocabulary and sentence structures for clarity, purpose and effect with accurate spelling and punctuation.	Builds skills for Component 2 NEA Questions 3, 5 and 6 Builds skills for Component 2 NEA writing tasks Questions 8 and 9	Builds skills for GCSE English Language Paper 1 Question 2 Language analysis and Question 5 (Narrative writing)

Topic 3 Fashion

Lesson	Assessment Objectives	Big question	
1 What is fashion?	AO1 Read and understand a range of texts: identify and interpret explicit and implicit information and ideas.	What is fashion?	
2 Work wear	AO3 Compare writers' ideas and perspectives.	Why do we have uniforms?	
3 What's the difference?	AO5 Communicate clearly, effectively and imaginatively, selecting and adapting tone, style and register for different forms, purposes and audiences AO6	Why are there different types of fashion text?	
4 Following fashion	AO1 AO2 Explain and comment on how writers use language and structure to achieve effects and influence readers, using relevant subject terminology to support views. AO6	How important is fashion to you?	
5 Fashion in the 19th century	AO1 Read and understand a range of texts: identify and interpret explicit and implicit information and ideas.	Is fashion so different today compared to 200 ago?	
6 Getting ready for a party	AO5 Organise information and ideas, using structural and grammatical features to support coherence and cohesion of texts. AO6	How might you get ready for different events?	
GCSE-ready extension tasks	**Assessment Objectives**	**NEA question types**	**How it helps prepare for GCSE**
Read and compare two passages from a modern story and a narrative based on a nineteenth-century novel (*Little Women*).	AO1 Read and understand a range of texts: identify and interpret explicit and implicit information and ideas. AO3 Compare writers' ideas and perspectives.	Builds skills for Component 2 NEA Questions 1, 2 and 4 Builds skills for Component 2 NEA Question 7	Builds skills for GCSE English Language Paper 1 and Paper 2 Question 1 (Comprehension) and Paper 2 Question 4 (Comparison)

Topic 4 Sport

Lesson	Assessment Objectives	Big question
1 Supporting a team or person	**AO1** Read and understand a range of texts: Identify and interpret explicit and implicit information and ideas. **AO8**	How do people support a particular sportsperson or team?
2 Rival supporters	**AO5** Communicate clearly, effectively and imaginatively, selecting and adapting tone, style and register for different forms, purposes and audiences.	How would you respond to a supporter of a rival team?
3 Making a match sound exciting	**AO2** Explain and comment on how writers use language and structure to achieve effects and influence readers, using relevant subject terminology to support views. **AO8**	How does a commentator make a match sound exciting?
4 The supporter's view	**AO3** Compare writers' ideas and perspectives. **AO7** **AO9**	How far can you trust a supporter's view of a match?
5 The perfect player	**AO5** Organise information and ideas, using structural and grammatical features to support coherence and cohesion of texts. **AO8**	What kind of players would make the perfect team?
6 How to be a sports writer	**AO6** Use vocabulary and sentence structures for clarity, purpose and effect, with accurate spelling and punctuation.	Can you be a sports writer?

GCSE-ready extension tasks	Assessment Objectives	NEA question types	How it helps prepare for GCSE
Reading, commenting on and comparing different viewpoints.	**AO2** Explain and comment on how writers use language and structure to achieve effects and influence readers, using relevant subject terminology to support views. **AO3** Compare writers' ideas and perspectives.	Builds skills for Component 2 NEA Questions 3, 5 and 6 Builds skills for Component 2 NEA Question 7	Builds skills for GCSE English Language Paper 2 Question 2 (Language analysis) and Question 4 (Comparison)

Component 2 Creative Writing & Reading

14 • Medium-term plans

© HarperCollins*Publishers* 2016

Topic 5 Transport

Lesson	Assessment Objectives	Big question
1 Full steam ahead	AO1 Read and understand a range of texts: identify and interpret explicit and implicit information and ideas.	What forms of transport are still powered by steam?
2 A traveller's diary	AO5 AO6 Use vocabulary and sentence structures for clarity, purpose and effect, with accurate spelling and punctuation.	What transport would you use to get to a big city?
3 The long cycle ride	AO1 AO2 Explain and comment on how writers use language and structure to achieve effects and influence readers, using relevant subject terminology to support views.	Could you ride from John O'Groats to Land's End?
4 Flying high	AO5 Organise information and ideas, using structural and grammatical features to support coherence and cohesion of texts.	What is it like flying in a helicopter?
5 Travelling to France	AO5 Communicate clearly, effectively and imaginatively, selecting and adapting tone, style and register for different forms, purposes and audiences. AO6	What are the different ways to get to France?
6 Cars in the future	AO5 AO6 Use vocabulary and sentence structures for clarity, purpose and effect, with accurate spelling and punctuation.	What will we be driving in 50 years time?

GCSE-ready extension tasks	Assessment Objectives	NEA question types	How it helps prepare for GCSE
Planning and writing a story using paragraphs and dialogue.	AO5 Communicate clearly, effectively and imaginatively, selecting and adapting tone, style and register for different forms, purposes and audiences. AO6 Use vocabulary and sentence structures for clarity, purpose and effect, with accurate spelling and punctuation.	Builds skills for Component 2 NEA writing tasks Questions 8 and 9	Builds skills for Paper 1 Question 5 (Narrative writing)

CELEBRITIES 1

'I want to be famous'

Assessment objectives
- **AO1** Read and understand a range of texts: Identify and interpret explicit and implicit information and ideas.
- **AO7** Demonstrate presentation skills.
- **AO8** Listen and respond appropriately to spoken language, including to questions and feedback on presentations.

Non-exam assessment
- Silver Step component 1
- Gold Step component 1

Differentiated learning outcomes
- **Entry Level 1 students** should recognise the major events of Lizzy Fame's life.
- **Entry Level 2 students** should recall specific details about Lizzy Fame's life.
- **Entry Level 3 students** should demonstrate an understanding of the main details of Lizzy Fame's life.
- **GCSE-ready students** should demonstrate a firm understanding of the significant points of Lizzy Fame's interview.

Resources
- **Worksheets**: 1.1, 1.2
- **PPT 1**: How does someone become famous?

Big question — *How does someone become famous?* Ask students for their initial thoughts. Prompt students' thinking by suggesting well-known celebrities and encouraging students to come up with aspects of their life that have contributed to their fame. Encourage students to think about whether they would like to be famous and for what.

Getting you thinking

As students enter the class, play the theme tune from *Britain's Got Talent*: www.youtube.com/watch?v=8oRqu6fSpGk.

Each student chooses their favourite celebrity. In pairs or small groups, they have to explain what their chosen celebrity has done to achieve their fame.

Display Slide 1 from **PPT 1**: How does someone become famous? Explain that, in this lesson, students will find out about a celebrity called Lizzy Fame. Ask students to look at the image on the board and then discuss how they think Lizzy Fame may have become a celebrity.

> **Give extra support** by...
> ...suggesting well-known celebrities (footballers, singers, etc.). Ask students what these people are known for by the public.
>
> **Give extra challenge** by...
> ...encouraging students to choose a controversial celebrity and explain why members of the public disagree about their fame.

Explore the skills

Explain that Lizzy Fame is being interviewed on the TV show, *Pop TV*. Check that students are familiar with a chat show format by asking them to give examples that they have seen.

Students read Lizzy Fame's interview on **Worksheet 1.1** and highlight anything that has helped her achieve her dream of becoming famous.

> **Give extra challenge by...**
>
> ...asking students to be prepared to explain what at least two of the details they have highlighted show about Lizzy Fame's character.

Develop the skills

Display Slide 2 of **PPT 1**. Use the slide to explain what is meant by a 'main/significant point', as set out in the level descriptors for AO1 and in the learning objectives for this lesson. Ask a confident student from the class to read out the points they have highlighted for the previous task. The rest of the class should use their thumbs to indicate how significant they consider each point to be: thumbs up = very significant; thumbs middle = quite significant; thumbs down = not significant.

Students complete **Worksheet 1.2**, which works in conjunction with **Worksheet 1.1**.

> **Give extra support by...**
> ...helping students to number the points they have underlined in chronological order, before starting on the worksheet.
>
> **Give extra challenge by...**
> ...asking students to justify which of the events of Lizzy Fame's life has contributed most towards her fame.

Apply the skills

Display Slide 3 of **PPT 1**. Check that learners are familiar with the term 'autobiography'. Give examples of the types of life events that are usually included in an autobiography.

Students work in groups to come up with a contents page of chapter headings for Lizzy Fame's autobiography. They can use their own words or use short quotations from her interview.

After a few minutes, students present their chapter headings to the other groups, explaining why they have chosen each of the chapter headings.

> **Give extra support by...**
> ...helping students to choose one word that sums up each event in Lizzy Fame's life.
>
> ...asking students to demonstrate from which section of the interview text they took inspiration for each chapter title.
>
> **Give extra challenge by...**
> ...encouraging students to create catchy, enticing chapter headings that might engage a potential audience.
>
> ...encouraging more able students to research biographies of celebrities they are interested in (using websites such as BBC Profile: www.bbc.co.uk/programmes/p0116mpt or www.biography.com) and to come up with chapter headings for these celebrities' autobiographies.

| **Big answer plenary** | Ask students to reconsider the Big Question: *How does someone become famous?* They should try and come up with their own responses to this question. If necessary, they can begin their answers with 'Lizzy Fame became famous because...' |

CELEBRITIES 2

What is it like to be a celebrity?

Assessment objectives
AO5 Communicate clearly, effectively and imaginatively, selecting and adapting tone, style and register for different forms, purposes and audiences.

Non-exam assessment
- Silver Step component 1
- Gold Step component 1

Differentiated learning outcomes
- **Entry Level 1 students** should sequence three related events in a diary and, with prompting, choose an appropriate writing style.
- **Entry Level 2 students** should sequence events in a diary using simple sequenced sentences and begin to demonstrate some simple adaptation of style.
- **Entry Level 3 students** should sequence events in a diary logically using grammatically correct sentences and demonstrate some evidence of adaptation of style.
- **GCSE-ready students** should sequence events in a diary in a sustained, developed and interesting way using an appropriate style.

Resources
- **Worksheets**: 2.1, 2.2
- **PPT 2**: A day in the life of a celebrity
- Individual whiteboards or plain paper

Big question — *What is a day in the life of a celebrity like?* Ask students to suggest ways in which their own daily routines might be different from those of a celebrity. Encourage them to explain which of these differences are due to the celebrity's fame and which are due to other factors (age, location, responsibilities, etc.). If possible, guide students to begin considering what they would like to do each day if they were famous.

Getting you thinking

Display Slide 1 of **PPT 2**: A day in the life of a celebrity. Explain that these pictures suggest some of the things that Lizzy Fame does on a typical day. Give students five minutes to discuss in groups what each of the images represents. Ask them to try to describe the events they have come up with in as much detail as possible.

Give extra support by...
...asking students to begin the discussions by simply describing what they see. Then help them to think about how the objects/scenes they have identified might fit into a day in the life of a singer.

Give extra challenge by...
...encouraging students to suggest what Lizzy Fame's attitudes to each of the events in her day might be: how much would she probably enjoy each one?

Explore the skills

Explain to students that they will be looking at how to write diary entries. Ask students to define a diary and to give examples of the types of details that a person may want to include in a diary. Explain the importance of chronological structure for a diary entry.

Ask students to pick three or four events that they would include in a diary entry about the previous day. Using paper or individual whiteboards, students draw a rough sketch to represent each of these events. This should take five to ten minutes. The class then have to guess what each other's drawings represent.

Give extra support by...
...encouraging students to consider what they have already done on the day of the lesson. If there are events that happen every day, this can provide a starting point for their sketches.

Give extra challenge by...
...asking students to imagine they were someone different (e.g. an astronaut, the Queen) and draw events for this person's life.

Develop the skills

Display Slide 2 from **PPT 2** and distribute **Worksheet 2.1**. Ask the class to read the first example of a diary entry. In pairs, allow students to discuss what is good about the diary entry and what could be improved.

Elicit students' opinions of the diary entry. Guide them to focus on the positive aspects of the text (clear sequencing, accurate simple sentences) and the aspects that could be improved (little development; impersonal style is inappropriate).

Display Slide 3 from **PPT 2**. Repeat the previous activity, looking at the second diary entry on the worksheet, and asking students to discuss in pairs what the positive and negative aspects of this text are. Students' responses should this time reflect the more appropriate personal style and greater level of detail, as well as criticising the lack of clear sequencing. Emphasise the importance of maintaining a clear chronological order in diary writing.

Give extra support by...
...helping students to number the points in the second diary entry in chronological order, i.e. the order they actually happened.

Give extra challenge by...
...asking students to rewrite the second diary to improve the sequencing of events, adding in linking phrases to improve the flow.

Apply the skills

Students imagine they are Lizzy Fame. Using the images from Slide 1 of the **PPT 2** and the details mentioned on Slide 2, students complete **Worksheet 2.2**, writing a diary entry to describe a typical day in Lizzy Fame's life. It may be necessary to review each of the three PPT slides to remind students of events they might include. Encourage students to include as much detail as possible and to write in an appropriate, personal style.

Give extra support by...
...asking students to look back at the sketches of their day and use these as a template. For each, ask the students whether this would be similar or different for Lizzy Fame. They can use their answers as the basis for their writing.

Give extra challenge by...
...encouraging students not to use the writing frame and to write their diary entry completely from scratch.

Big answer plenary	Ask students to reconsider the Big Question: *What is a day in the life of a celebrity like?* They should be able to give examples of events that might occur in the life of a celebrity and explain how far this differs from their own lives.

CELEBRITIES 3

Celebrities in the 19th century

Assessment objectives
AO1 Read and understand a range of texts: Identify and interpret explicit and implicit information and ideas.
AO9 Use spoken English effectively in speeches and presentations.

Non-exam assessment
- **Silver Step** component 1
- **Gold Step** component 1

Differentiated learning outcomes
- **Entry Level 1 students** should make simple inferences about Florence Nightingale's achievements.
- **Entry Level 2 students** should make simple inferences about Florence Nightingale's achievements, perhaps supported by textual detail.
- **Entry Level 3 students** should make inferences about Florence Nightingale's achievements, based on specific textual details.
- **GCSE-ready students** should make inferences about Nightingale's significant achievements, referring to the text to support their views.

Resources
- **Worksheets**: 3.1, 3.2
- **PPT 3**: Celebrities in the 19th century

Big question — *What kind of celebrities were there in the 19th century?* Ask students to recap examples of celebrities they have already thought about during the topic. Then challenge them to think about whether similar celebrities could have existed in Victorian times.

Getting you thinking

Give extra support by...
...showing students a clip from a medical drama (such as BBC's *Casualty*) featuring nurses.

Give extra challenge by...
...encouraging students to think about how a nurse's job may have changed over the years.

Display Slide 1 of **PPT 3**: Celebrities in the 19th century. Ask students to come up with words that they associate with nurses. Ask if any of the students have met a nurse. If so, ask them to explain what kind of people they were and what kind of tasks they carried out; if not, draw out what expectations students would have of nurses.

In groups or as a class, students discuss the main tasks a nurse has to carry out and the qualities they think a nurse needs. They can use **Worksheet 3.1** as a stimulus, as appropriate. Students may benefit from using the Speaking and Listening framework (see Appendix 1 at the end of this pack).

Explore the skills

Display Slide 2 of **PPT 3**. Tell the students that this shows Florence Nightingale and that she was famous for the improvements she made to nursing. Explain that she became a nurse when the profession was not well respected, but through her achievements and innovations she made nurses far more appreciated. Explain that she made many improvements to the design of hospitals and that she founded the first professional training school for nurses in 1860.

From this information, ask students to explain to each other what effect Nightingale had on the 19th-century public's view of nursing.

> **Give extra support by...**
> ...providing sentence starters for students to frame their responses, such as 'Florence Nightingale made people think nurses were...' and 'Florence Nightingale made hospitals better by...'
>
> **Give extra challenge by...**
> ...asking students to use websites such as www.florence-nightingale.co.uk to research further information about Florence Nightingale.

Develop the skills

Help students read through the fact file on **Worksheet 3.2**. It illustrates some of Florence Nightingale's notable achievements and examples of how she became a celebrity of the Victorian era. Check students' understanding of key words.

Lead students through the first question on the worksheet as a class, demonstrating how to infer that Nightingale's determination to be a nurse made her stand out from her peers. Students complete the rest of the worksheet independently, inferring the impact of Nightingale's achievements from the textual details that have been highlighted.

> **Give extra support by...**
> ...encouraging students to rephrase the textual detail in their own words, thereby demonstrating understanding, if not sophisticated inference.
>
> **Give extra challenge by...**
> ...asking students to underline the key words or phrases within the textual detail that has led them to their inference.

Apply the skills

Display Slide 3 of **PPT 3**. Ask students to plan a 30-second speech for a group of primary school children explaining how Nightingale changed the nursing profession in the 19th century. They should use **Worksheets 3.1** and **3.2** to help them with their ideas. Encourage students to display the skills of a good speech: speaking slowly and clearly; maintaining eye contact with their audience; using gestures to emphasise key points etc. Give students 10 minutes planning time and then five minutes practice time. Students should then deliver their speeches to a familiar adult or small familiar group (EL1), a familiar group (EL2) or the rest of the class (EL3/GCSE-ready).

> **Give extra support by...**
> ...asking students to explain some of the differences between nursing before Florence Nightingale and nursing today.
>
> **Give extra challenge by...**
> ...challenging students to make their speeches entertaining for a young audience.

Big answer plenary	Ask students to reconsider the Big Question: *What kind of celebrities were there in the 19th century?* All students should be able to cite Florence Nightingale as an example of a 19th-century celebrity, with some being able to explain what it was that made her so famous.

CELEBRITIES 4
Do some people deserve to be famous?

Assessment objectives
- **AO4** Evaluate texts and support this with appropriate textual references.
- **AO8** Listen and respond appropriately to spoken language, including to questions and feedback on presentations.

Non-exam assessment
- Silver Step component 1
- Gold Step component 1

Differentiated learning outcomes
- **Entry Level 1 students** should make simple statements of their own views about whether people deserve fame.
- **Entry Level 2 students** should make simple statements of their own views about whether people deserve fame, supporting them with reasons.
- **Entry Level 3 students** should express their own views about whether people deserve fame, with some reference to evidence.
- **GCSE-ready students** should assess the extent to which they agree or disagree with others' views about whether people deserve to be celebrities, using textual details for support.

Resources
- **Worksheets**: 4.1, 4.2, 4.3
- **PPT 4**: Do some people deserve to be famous?

Big question | *Do some people deserve to be famous?* Ask students to give examples of celebrities with whom they are familiar. Challenge them to justify whether their chosen celebrities deserve to be famous. Encourage other students to put forward counter-arguments to stimulate discussion.

Getting you thinking

Give extra challenge by…
…asking more able students to take up a position that represents a viewpoint that differs from their own and getting them to explain why some other people may hold this view.

Display Slide 1 of **PPT 4**. Through whole-class questioning, establish who each of the people shown on the slide are and the primary reason why they are a celebrity. Ask all students to stand and line up in the middle of the room. Say to the class: 'I believe Wayne Rooney deserves to be famous.' Students have to move to a position in their room to show how far they agree with this statement – standing by the right-hand wall signifies total agreement, standing by the left-hand wall represents total disagreement. Encourage students to explain why they have positioned themselves where they are. Facilitate discussion between students who disagree by asking them to justify their views.

Explore the skills

Display Slide 2 of **PPT 4**. Ask students what they already know about Malala Yousafzai and Harry Styles. In groups, students should discuss who they believe deserves to be the more famous of the two. They should be prepared to give reasons for their views.

Students then vote on which person they believe deserves to be more of a celebrity.

Give extra support by…
… helping less able students to describe why Yousafzai and Styles are famous and then say whether these are good or bad reasons to be a celebrity.

> **Give extra challenge** by…
> …encouraging students to suggest ways in which either person could become more (or less) deserving of their celebrity status.

Develop the skills

Explain that the Nobel Peace Prize rewards those who work for unity between different people across the world.

As a class, read through **Worksheet 4.1**, asking students to highlight key points in the fact file. Students should then swap worksheets and take it in turns to ask each other whether they feel the points that have been highlighted make Harry Styles and/or Malala Yousafzai deserving of celebrity status. Students can use the questions at the bottom of the worksheet to help them.

> **Give extra support** by…
> …asking students to think about why they highlighted the point in the first place – what it was about the detail that they thought was important – rather than evaluating how far it makes the individual deserving of fame.
>
> **Give extra challenge** by…
> …asking students to ask their own open questions to encourage their interviewee to elaborate on their views.

Apply the skills

Show the class extracts from interviews with Harry Styles and Malala Yousafzai (www.youtube.com/watch?v=QrnYXM9Rt7E and www.youtube.com/watch?v=NKckKStggSY).
Ask the students whether these have changed their views.

Display Slide 3 of **PPT 4**. Divide the class in two and assign one half to Harry Styles and one half to Malala Yousafzai. Explain that students have 10 minutes in their groups to refine their arguments for why 'their' celebrity is more deserving of fame than the other. Students can use the information on **Worksheet 4.1** to help them, as well as the words provided on **Worksheet 4.3** for EL1/EL2. They should also use planning **Worksheet 4.2**, as a group, to prepare for a debate.

Stage a debate between the two sides of the class, allowing each to state their arguments in turn and encouraging students to respond to each other's arguments sensitively and thoughtfully, using evidence where possible.

At the end of the debate, ask students to vote again on who is more deserving of their fame, Harry Styles or Malala Yousafzai. Discuss any changes from the first vote, asking students to explain why they have changed their minds, if applicable.

> **Give extra support** by…
> …asking students to respond to others' arguments using the starter, 'I agree because…' or 'I disagree because…'
>
> **Give extra challenge** by…
> …encouraging students to research more information about Yousafzai's life, using websites such as www.malala.org/malalas-story .

| Big answer plenary | Ask students to reconsider the Big Question: *Do some people deserve to be famous?* Get students to articulate a response to this question, using one of the examples they have looked at in the lesson. |

CELEBRITIES 5: What would you like to be famous for?

Assessment objectives

AO5 Organise information and ideas, using structural and grammatical features to support coherence and cohesion of texts.

Non-exam assessment
- Silver Step component 1
- Gold Step component 1

Differentiated learning outcomes
- **Entry Level 1 students** should sometimes arrange ideas about their fictional celebrity life in appropriate order.
- **Entry Level 2 students** should state ideas about their fictional celebrity life in simple sequenced sentences.
- **Entry Level 3 students** should sequence ideas about their fictional celebrity life logically, with a clear beginning, middle and end.
- **GCSE-ready students** should sequence ideas about their fictional celebrity life in a sustained, developed and interesting way.

Resources
- **Worksheets**: 5.1, 5.2, 5.3
- **PPT 5**: What would you be famous for?

Big question *If you were a celebrity, what would you be famous for?* Suggest to students that everyone is good at something, whether it's caring for others, being creative, excelling at sport, etc. Guide students to identify what their talent might be and how this might lead to becoming a celebrity. If students are unsure, they can decide what they would really love to be famous for.

Getting you thinking

Display Slide 1 of **PPT 5** to set the scene. Ask students to imagine what life would be like if they were a world-famous celebrity. Allow a confident student to sit at the front of the room and be 'hot-seated' by the rest of the class, with students asking them to describe details about their life as a celebrity.

> **Give extra support** by…
> …providing students with the guidance questions on **Worksheet 5.1**.
>
> **Give extra challenge** by…
> …asking more able students to challenge the hot-seated student about aspects of their imaginary life and suggest alternatives to the celebrity lifestyle they have envisaged.

Explore the skills

Give students 10 minutes to complete **Worksheet 5.2** in as much detail as possible, further developing the details of their celebrity life. Encourage students to write in full, simple sentences as much as possible.

Display Slide 2 of **PPT 5**. Silver: Explain to students how adding 'because…' can add detail to their sentences. Gold: Explain to students that including subordinate clauses in sentences is a way of adding more information and, therefore, developing ideas. As appropriate, guide students to add simple phrases (EL1) or subordinate clauses (EL2 & EL3) to the simple sentences they have written on **Worksheet 5.2**, in order to develop their ideas further.

Give extra support by...
...allowing students initially to write single words on **Worksheet 5.2**, then showing them how to add short subordinate clauses starting with 'which' to expand their ideas.

Give extra challenge by...
...encouraging students to suggest ways in which their celebrity lives would be both positive and negative.

Develop the skills

Display Slide 3 of **PPT 5**. As a class, read through the postcard from Tina, a friend from school. Give students three minutes in pairs to discuss which of the ideas from **Worksheet 5.2** they would include in a reply to Tina.

Ask students to number the statements they have written on the worksheet in the order in which they will write about them.

Give extra support by...
...suggesting questions to which Tina might want the answer ('Where do you live?', 'What do you do in your spare time?', etc.) and helping students find suitable responses on their worksheets.

Give extra challenge by...
...asking students to suggest suitable connectives that will allow them to link their ideas together in a coherent and interesting way.

Apply the skills

Allow students 10–15 minutes to write a short letter or postcard in response to Tina, telling her about their life as a celebrity. EL1 & EL2 students can use **Worksheet 5.3** as scaffolding. Encourage them to include subordinate clauses to develop their ideas and to maintain the structure that they have planned out on **Worksheet 5.2**.

In pairs, students share their work with each other, discussing how well they have structured the aspects of their fictional celebrity life: simply, logically or interestingly. Each student should suggest one way in which the structure of their partner's work could be improved.

Give extra support by...
...encouraging students to follow the structure of Tina's postcard, substituting details of their made-up life.

Give extra challenge by...
...encouraging students to adopt an appropriate, informal tone and to try to incorporate humour in order to engage Tina.

...asking students to research the daily life of a famous person, using sources such as www.huffingtonpost.com/2014/07/09/daily-routines-of-famous-creatives_n_5571536.html – encourage them to try to find similarities or links between the lives of famous people.

| **Big answer plenary** | Ask students to reconsider the Big Question: *If you were a celebrity, what would you be famous for?* Ask students to get into different pairs from those in which they have been working previously. Partners explain their responses to the Big Question to each other, demonstrating how their chosen path to celebrity would result in the life they have described in their correspondence with Tina. |

CELEBRITIES 6: Should we ever feel sorry for celebrities?

Assessment objectives
- **AO6** Use vocabulary and sentence structures for clarity, purpose and effect, with accurate spelling and punctuation.
- **AO7** Demonstrate presentation skills.
- **AO9** Use spoken English effectively in speeches and presentations.

Non-exam assessment
- Silver Step component 1
- Gold Step component 1

Differentiated learning outcomes
- **Entry Level 1 students** should describe a scene using simple description and some awareness of full stops and capital letters.
- **Entry Level 2 students** should describe a scene using appropriate adjectives and using full stops and capital letters.
- **Entry Level 3 students** should describe a scene using words for variety and interest and using full stops and capital letters.
- **GCSE-ready students** should describe a scene using effective and adventurous description and beginning to use punctuation within sentences.

Resources
- **Worksheets**: 6.1, 6.2, 6.3
- **PPT 6**: Should we ever feel sorry for celebrities?

Big question — *Should we ever feel sorry for celebrities?* Ask students to think of any aspects of celebrities' lives that might be negative. Encourage them to suggest real-life examples of scandals, high-profile break-ups and other instances where they have felt sympathy towards a celebrity.

Getting you thinking

Display Slide 1 of **PPT 6**. In groups, students discuss what the stories might be behind the headlines about Lizzy Fame. Ask them to choose the story idea that they feel will provoke the most sympathy from the public.

Tell students they are going to imagine they work as a journalist. They are going to need to persuade the editor to run their story. Ask students to suggest persuasive techniques and write their suggestions on the board. Examples include:

- Use powerful verbs and strong adjectives.
- Ask rhetorical questions.
- Give quotations.
- Repeat key points.
- Add some facts.
- Use linking words ('therefore', 'for this reason', 'that is why...').
- Summarise your arguments.

Give students five minutes to plan a group presentation to the editor of their paper, persuading the editor that their story will trigger sympathy from the public and should therefore be run on the front page.

> **Give extra support** by...
> ...guiding students to present the facts of the story as they envisage it, rather than focusing on persuading the editor about its potential effect on readers.
>
> **Give extra challenge** by...
> ...asking more able students to come up with a completely original story, not suggested by the headlines on the PPT, to pitch to the newspaper editor.

Explore the skills

Display Slide 2 of **PPT 6**. In pairs, and using **Worksheet 6.1**, students discuss and note down all the different words they might use to describe the scene, under the following headings: What can you see? What can you hear? How do you feel?

Through class discussion, share students' ideas and encourage them to add to their own list of words. Ask students to write three correctly punctuated phrases (EL1) or sentences (EL2 and EL3), each containing one of the words from their list.

> **Give extra challenge** by...
> ...encouraging students to think of words inspired by the other senses (smell, touch, taste) to add interest and variety to their descriptions.

Develop the skills

Read through **Worksheet 6.2** with students, checking they understand the text. Discuss the meaning of the word 'paparazzi' and explore the reputation of paparazzi among the students and the public. Allow students 10 minutes to rewrite the text on **Worksheet 6.2**, correcting the punctuation and highlighting effective vocabulary.

> **Give extra support** by...
> ...asking students to use a different coloured pen to mark the original text on **Worksheet 6.2**, rather than asking them to rewrite the text.
>
> **Give extra challenge** by...
> ...encouraging students to substitute adventurous and effective description to improve the original text.

Apply the skills

Display Slide 3 of **PPT 6**. Allow students five minutes to begin writing a script for a one-minute speech arguing for or against the statement: 'Celebrities should be treated more fairly.' EL1 and EL2 students can use **Worksheet 6.3** to structure their plans.

At the end of the allotted time, ask students to swap their work so far with a partner and mark each other's work for errors, paying particular attention to punctuation. Ask students to give each other one target for how to improve. Then allow students a further 5–10 minutes to finish their speeches. Encourage students to read their speeches to a trusted adult (EL1), trusted group (EL2) or the class (EL3/GCSE-ready) as appropriate, and facilitate feedback.

> **Give extra support** by...
> ...asking students to write a description of the paparazzi scene rather than an argumentative speech.
>
> **Give extra challenge** by...
> ...encouraging students to include a vivid, engaging description in their speech to support their arguments.
>
> ...encouraging students to explore issues around a right to privacy, using sites such as www.debate.org/opinions/do-celebrities-have-a-right-to-privacy . They then write their own argument as to whether famous people deserve private lives.

Big answer plenary	Ask students to reconsider the Big Question: *Should we ever feel sorry for celebrities?* Ask students to identify whether any of the speeches they have heard have influenced their views of this question.

DETECTIVES 1
The skills of a good detective

Assessment objectives

AO1 Read and understand a range of texts: identify and interpret explicit and implicit information and ideas.

AO7 Demonstrate presentation skills.

AO9 Use spoken English effectively in speeches and presentations.

Non-exam assessment
- Silver Step component 1
- Gold Step component 1

Differentiated learning outcomes
- **Entry Level 1 students** should locate some points and information in simple crime report.
- **Entry Level 2 students** should locate main points and information in a crime report.
- **Entry Level 3 students** should locate key points in a crime report.
- **GCSE-ready students** should locate and use ideas and information in a crime report.

Resources
- **Worksheets**: 1.1, 1.2
- **PPT 1**: Being a detective

Big question — *What skills do you need to be a detective?* Ask students what the word 'detective' means and draw out a definition that all the class are happy with. Given that a detective's job is to solve crimes, facilitate class discussion about what skills they will need.

Getting you thinking

Display Slide 1 of **PPT 1**. Find out if any students can provide examples of detectives from books, television or film. As a class, explore what characteristics and skills these people have in common.

Each student chooses their favourite detective from those that have been mentioned in their discussion. In groups of four, students spend three minutes explaining why they believe their detective is particularly effective at solving crimes.

Give extra support by…
…suggesting famous detectives (Sherlock Holmes, Inspector Gadget, etc.) and helping students to explore how they carry out their occupation.

Give extra challenge by…
…asking students to rank the detectives that have been mentioned in order of effectiveness, making sure they are prepared to justify their decisions.

Explore the skills

Display Slide 2 from **PPT 1**. Explain that a valuable solid gold Egyptian statue has been stolen from the British Museum. Run through the key information of the crime. Tell students that police suspect the manager of the museum, Ms Sneer, of committing the crime, but they are not sure. Students should imagine they are the force's most trusted detective, Inspector Snoop, who has been asked to investigate.

Inspector Snoop is about to interview Ms Sneer. Distribute **Worksheet 1.1** and ask each student to do the first task on the worksheet, which involves composing questions they could ask Ms Sneer about the details of the crime.

Give extra support by...
...guiding students to focus on when the crime occurred, what equipment would have been used and what skills the criminal would have needed.

Give extra challenge by...
...asking them to explore Ms Sneer's possible motivations for the crime by probing into her life.

Develop the skills

Pretend to be Ms Sneer and allow students to question you about the crime. In your answers, reveal the following details to students:

- The museum normally opens between 9 a.m. and 5 p.m. on Wednesdays but was closed on Wednesday 13 July until 11 a.m., as you were not available to open it. You were somewhere else.
- You know a great deal about Egyptian artefacts, as you worked at the Egypt museum in Cairo for 20 years.
- You are a keen mountaineer and have lots of experience climbing. You keep your climbing equipment in your garage.
- You have not had a holiday in 10 years. Your life-long dream is to take a month-long tour of the desert in Egypt, but you have never been able to afford it.

Encourage students to make notes of important details they find out about Ms Sneer on the second part of **Worksheet 1.1**.

Give extra support by...
...stepping out of role to suggest which details of your responses as Ms Sneer students should note down to focus on later.

Give extra challenge by...
...answering any closed questions as briefly as possible to encourage students to ask open, exploratory questions.

Apply the skills

Give students **Worksheet 1.2**. They should highlight any important details of Henry the cleaner's diary that they believe help build a case against Ms Sneer.

Display Slide 3 of **PPT 1**. Ask each student to plan a one-minute presentation to be delivered to a judge arguing that Ms Sneer is guilty of the theft. Allow students 10 minutes planning time. Encourage them to include details from **Worksheets 1.1** and **1.2**.

Students deliver their presentations. Feed back to each student, highlighting where they have used details from the worksheets and assessing their use of spoken English.

Give extra support by...
...asking less able students to summarise the details of the case, rather than persuading the judge.

Give extra challenge by...
...encouraging students to use inference to suggest possible motives for the crime.

Big answer plenary	Ask students to reconsider the Big Question: *What skills do you need to be a detective?* Students should think back over the activities within the lesson and complete the statement: 'One of the skills a detective might need is...'

DETECTIVES 2

Could you be a detective?

Assessment objectives

AO5 Communicate clearly, effectively and imaginatively, selecting and adapting tone, style and register for different forms, purposes and audiences.

Controlled assessment
- Silver Step component 1
- Gold Step component 1

Differentiated learning outcomes
- **Entry Level 1 students** should inconsistently match writing to structure in their applications.
- **Entry Level 2 students** should show some awareness of the non-narrative form in their applications.
- **Entry Level 3 students** should sometimes adapt writing style to match the purpose of their applications.
- **GCSE-ready students** should organise writing appropriately for the purpose of their applications.

Resources
- **Worksheets**: 2.1, 2.2, 2.3
- **PPT 2**: Could you be a detective?

Big question — *Could you be a detective?* Recap on Lesson 1 and ask students which aspects of a detective's job appeal to them. Explore what type of selection procedures they would expect in the recruitment of a new detective.

Getting you thinking

Display Slide 1 from **PPT 2**. Ask students if they have ever been to a job interview, or, if not, what they expect from a job interview. Explore the importance of making a good impression and draw out the ways in which people might achieve that. Students can use the prompts on the slide as necessary.

In groups, students agree three tips for interviewees and note them down, explaining how to make the best impression at an interview.

> **Give extra support by…**
> …asking students to imagine similarly pressurised situations they may have experienced (e.g. talking to a head teacher) and explore how they tried to give a good impression.
>
> **Give extra challenge by…**
> …encouraging students to create tableaux representing good impressions and bad impressions in an interview situation.

Explore the skills

Tell the students to imagine they are going to be interviewed for the job of detective. Ask the class to feed back questions that they might expect to be asked and possible responses to these. Challenge students to express their responses in an appropriate register for a job interview.

Students complete **Worksheet 2.1**, adapting or selecting the register of the responses to make them more appropriate and suggesting responses to subsequent questions.

Give extra support by...
...encouraging students to verbalise their responses to each other, refining them until they are appropriate, before asking them to write on the worksheet.

Give extra challenge by...
...urging students to develop a character voice in their responses.

Develop the skills

Display Slide 2 of **PPT 2**. Read through it with the students and explain that they are going to apply for the job of detective. Distribute **Worksheet 2.2** and read through the adverts with the group or class. (The adverts are slightly different for each level, so you will need to be flexible here and possibly read through the different adverts with different groups of students.)

Students complete the worksheet, using dictionaries as necessary to find the definitions of the key attributes of a detective and suggesting examples of experiences from their own lives that demonstrate these attributes. Alternatively, they can create a new character for themselves who is going to apply for the job. Allow students 5 to 10 minutes for this activity.

Give extra support by...
...scaffolding students' statements for each of the attributes with the structure, 'I am a _____ person, because I _____'.

Apply the skills

Tell students that they are now going to write a letter of application to answer the detective advert. Display Slide 2 of **PPT 2** again. Hand out **Worksheet 2.3**. Talk through the sentence starters (Silver level students only) and explain how these can be used to start phrases (EL1), simple sentences (EL2), sequenced sentences (EL3) or paragraphs (GCSE-Ready) in the letter of application. Verbally model how to use the responses from **Worksheet 2.1** and the experiences from **Worksheet 2.2** to create detailed paragraphs. Encourage students to maintain an appropriate register in their responses.

Give students up to 15 minutes to complete their letters of application, using **Worksheet 2.3** as a writing frame.

Talk through the sentence starters (Silver level students only) and explain how these can be used to start the paragraphs in the letter of application. Verbally model how to use the responses from Worksheet 2.1 and the experiences from Worksheet 2.2 to create detailed paragraphs. Encourage..." Should read: "

Give extra support by...
...encouraging Silver level students to add their own words in right-hand column of **Worksheet 2.3**.

Give extra challenge by...
...encouraging students to use characterisation, as well as an appropriate register, throughout their letters of application.

Big answer plenary	Ask students to reconsider the Big Question: *Could you be a detective?* In pairs, students should explain one aspect of their character that they feel would make them a good detective.

DETECTIVES

3

Crime in the 19th century

Assessment objectives
AO1   Read and understand a range of texts: identify and interpret explicit and implicit information and ideas.
AO8   Listen and respond appropriately to spoken language, including to questions and feedback on presentations.

Non-exam assessment
- Silver Step component 1
- Gold Step component 1

Differentiated learning outcomes
- **Entry Level 1 students** should be able to make a simple prediction about a suspect.
- **Entry Level 2 students** should make a prediction about a suspect based on an event.
- **Entry Level 3 students** should make predictions about a suspect's actions and motives.
- **GCSE-ready students** should make inferences and deductions based on a suspect's actions and events in a text.

Resources
- **Worksheets**: 3.1, 3.2
- **PPT 3**: What kind of crimes did detectives have to solve in the 19th century?
- Access to ICT
- Dictionaries

Big question | *What kind of crimes did detectives have to solve in the 19th century? Ask students to list as many crimes as they can think of that a detective might be asked to solve today. For each one, challenge students to consider whether the crime would have existed in the 19th century and, if it did, how it would be different.*

Getting you thinking

Display Slide 1 from **PPT 3**. Read out the prompting questions and allow students to think for one minute about their responses. They then share these responses with a partner to try to expand their responses.

Explain that this is a hansom cab, which was the Victorian equivalent of a black taxi. They were one of the ways that people got around London in the 19th century. Explain that there were also horse buses and horse trams that were cheaper. Show students this video clip: www.youtube.com/watch?v=_8NPi5RSmI8 to engage them with the idea of horse-drawn transport.

> **Give extra support** by…
> …asking students to think about any words they can use to name any of the items in the picture, rather than focusing on the carriage as a whole.
>
> **Give extra challenge** by…
> …asking students to consider what types of crimes may have been linked to hansom cabs in Victorian times.

Explore the skills

Display Slide 2 from **PPT 2.3** and read through the fact file on horses in Victorian London with the students. If appropriate, allow them to read it individually.

Ask students to close their eyes and test their ability to recall details of the fact file by asking them the following questions about London's Victorian transport:

1. How many horses were used for London transport in Victorian times?
2. How much were horses worth?
3. What type of punishments could horse thieves expect to face?

4. How old was Frank Marsh when he was convicted of stealing a horse?

> **Give extra support** by…
> …highlighting key details from the fact file before asking the questions.
> …allowing students 10 seconds to look at the fact file again after question 2.

Develop the skills

Tell students that they are going to imagine they are a Victorian detective. A horse has been stolen on Millpond Street, central London. The hansom cab driver had tied up his horse while he went in for his lunch. When he came out, the horse was gone.

Ask students to read the information on **Worksheet 3.1**. Each student should decide which of the suspects is the most likely to be the horse thief.

Put students into groups of three or four and ask them to discuss the suspects for three minutes. Each group should try to reach a unanimous decision as to which of the suspects is likely to have stolen the horse from the hansom cab. They must be able to provide at least two reasons for their decision. If necessary, provide students with a Speaking and Listening framework (see Appendix 1 at the back of the book).

> **Give extra support** by…
> …highlighting key words in the details of the suspects and helping students to look them up in a dictionary.
>
> **Give extra challenge** by…
> …asking students to suggest one question they would ask each of the suspects in order to feel more confident in their selection of the most likely suspect.

Apply the skills

Assist the class in reading through the text on **Worksheet 3.2a** and guide them to highlight key details that provide evidence for how the horse theft has affected Bob, the hansom cab driver. Discuss how Bob seems to be feeling and explore which particular aspects of language communicate these feelings.

Ask students to discuss the question: 'How has Bob the hansom cab driver been affected by the horse theft?' Allow students 10 minutes to write their answers to the questions on **Worksheet 3.2b**.

Ask students to share their work with a partner and indicate which pieces of language from the passage have influenced their response.

> **Give extra challenge** by…
> …encouraging students to include inferences about the causes of Bob's feelings towards the police and other people trying to recover Bess.

| **Big answer plenary** | Ask students to reconsider the Big Question: *What kind of crimes did detectives have to solve in the 19th century?* Revisit students' initial thoughts about differences between crimes in the 19th century and today and explore whether their views have changed. |

DETECTIVES 4

Do detectives just investigate crimes?

Assessment objectives
AO4 Evaluate texts and support this with appropriate textual references.

Non-exam assessment
- Silver Step component 1
- Gold Step component 1

Differentiated learning outcomes
- **Entry Level 1 students** should make simple comments about the existence of the Loch Ness Monster.
- **Entry Level 2 students** should make simple comments about the existence of the Loch Ness Monster, sometimes supported by reasons.
- **Entry Level 3 students** should make comments about the writer's views of the Loch Ness Monster, sometimes supported by details.
- **GCSE-ready students** should express personal comments about the writer's views of the Loch Ness Monster, supported by appropriate details.

Resources
- **Worksheets**: 4.1, 4.2
- **PPT 4**: Do detectives just investigate crimes?
- Access to ICT

Big question — *Do detectives just investigate crimes?* Ask students to think of any mysteries that do not involve crimes. Draw out examples of conspiracy theories that students may have read about or seen on television. Begin to explore how the detective skills they have thought about so far in the unit might be useful in these situations.

Getting you thinking

Display Slide 1 from **PPT 4**. Discuss how each of the images might relate to the work of a detective. Questions to lead the discussion might include:

- What needs to be investigated in this situation?
- What conclusions might a detective or investigator hope to reach in this situation?
- How important is it that this situation is investigated?

Give extra support by…
…asking students to consider how much about what had happened would be known at the outset of each situation. Then ask them to consider what someone might want to find out.

Give extra challenge by…
…encouraging students to justify the amount of resources that should be devoted to investigating each of the situations suggested by the images.

Explore the skills

Display Slide 2 from **PPT 4**. Elicit from students what else they may know about the Loch Ness Monster. Allow more able students to research the Loch Ness Monster using sites such as www.nessie.co.uk .

In groups, students organise their ideas under two headings: 'Facts' and 'Myths'. Share the work between groups, exploring any discrepancies between different groups' classification of details as 'Facts' or 'Myths'.

Ask students to vote on whether they believe the Loch Ness Monster exists.

> **Give extra challenge** by…
> …asking students to suggest ways in which the 'Myths' they have come up with could be investigated and the circumstances under which they would be prepared to reclassify them as 'Facts'.

Develop the skills

Explain that one technique that detectives often use to solve mysteries is to look for patterns in information provided by witnesses. Ask the class to identify any common features in the information they have already explored in the lesson.

Students complete **Worksheet 4.1**. Encourage students to refer to specific details in the pictures to justify their views, either verbally or in writing, as appropriate.

> **Give extra support** by…
> …asking students to circle or list the similarities and differences between the images on the sheet.
>
> **Give extra challenge** by…
> …asking students to suggest reasons (other than the actual existence of the monster) why there might be similarities between the images that people have created.

Apply the skills

Display Slide 3 of **PPT 4**. Assist the class in reading through the text of **Worksheet 4.2** and guide the students to highlight key details that suggest the witness is convinced that he was not mistaken in what he saw.

Evaluate the student's statement that, given how convincing the witness's eyewitness account is, they believe that the Loch Ness Monster does exist (EL3 Gold). Allow students 15 minutes to complete their answer, helping them to pick out details that both question and support the reliability of the sighting.

Ask students to vote again on whether they believe the Loch Ness Monster exists. Explore why any students may have changed their minds, asking them to justify their views, referring to details in their own work.

> **Give extra support** by…
> …assisting students to express their own opinions about whether they believe the eyewitness and exploring which particular aspects of the account they find particularly convincing.
>
> **Give extra challenge** by…
> …supporting students to produce a balanced evaluation, considering possible motivations for the witness to make their account as convincing as possible.

Big answer plenary	Ask students to reconsider the Big Question: *Do detectives just investigate crimes?* Students should consider how the investigation they have carried out in this lesson compares to previous lessons in the unit.

DETECTIVES 5

What makes detectives exciting?

Assessment objectives
AO5 Organise information and ideas, using structural and grammatical features to support coherence and cohesion of texts.

Non-exam assessment
- Silver Step component 1
- Gold Step component 1

Differentiated learning outcomes
- **Entry Level 1 students** should arrange some events of a detective case in an appropriate order.
- **Entry Level 2 students** should describe the events of a detective case in simple sequenced sentences.
- **Entry Level 3 students** should describe the events of a detective case in logical, grammatically correct sentences.
- **GCSE-ready students** should describe the events of a detective case in developed and interesting ways, linking ideas with connectives.

Resources
- **Worksheets**: 5.1, 5.2
- **PPT 5**: What makes detectives exciting?
- Individual whiteboards

Big question — *What makes detectives exciting?* First, ask students to think of one or more exciting situations and to consider what makes them exciting. Then give students two minutes to sketch an exciting situation on individual whiteboards. It can be with or without a detective. They then have to explain to the rest of the class what makes their particular tableau exciting. Through this, draw out the ideas of peril and tension and the ways these might be created.

Getting you thinking

Display Slide 1 from **PPT 5**. In groups, students should discuss how the events might be linked together in a case to be solved by a detective. They should also discuss how a detective would discover the details surrounding each event. They then put them in chronological order.

For each event, students should write single words/phrases/sentences (depending on ability), describing it in as much detail as they are able.

Give extra support by…
…asking students simply to rewrite the sentences accompanying each image, adding in a single adjective.

Give extra challenge by…
…asking students also to rank the events in order of how much excitement they would evoke in someone reading about the case.

Explore the skills

Assist students to read the text of **Worksheet 5.1**. Explain that this text is based on the conclusion of a book by Agatha Christie, called *The Mysterious Affair at Styles*. The book features the detective Hercule Poirot and, at this point in the narrative, he is revealing who the murderer is.

Students complete the worksheet, putting the events mentioned in the text in sequence.

Give extra support by...

...asking students to summarise verbally the main incidents of the case, rather than expecting them to place them in chronological order on the timeline.

Give extra challenge by...

...asking students to highlight the points in the passage that suggest the assembled people listening to Poirot are excited (EL3 Gold).

Develop the skills

Display Slide 2 of **PPT 5**. Explain that you are going to look at another book written by crime writer Agatha Christie featuring a case solved by Poirot, *The Murder of Roger Ackroyd*. Also explain that this case involves lots of details and that Poirot waits a long time before revealing who the killer is. Students complete **Worksheet 5.2**, ordering the events of the case in a plausible chronological order. They should explain, verbally or in writing depending on their level, why they have chosen that order.

In pairs, students compare their sequencing of the plot events and discuss which order would create the most tension and excitement.

Give extra support by...

...helping students to sort the events into those that may have happened earlier and those that probably happened later.

Give extra challenge by...

...asking students to place the events in the order they should be revealed to readers in order to create the most excitement and tension.

Apply the skills

Display Slide 3 of **PPT 5**. Tell students to imagine that they are journalists writing for a local newspaper known for its sensational style and with a strong desire to engage and excite its readership. Students should come up with a catchy headline and at least three subheadings for a newspaper article exploring the case of Roger Ackroyd's murder. They should focus on the most intriguing and exciting details of the case. Allow students up to 15 minutes to write their headline and subheadings.

Give extra support by...

...asking students to write a phrase stating one of the events, for each of the subheadings.

Give extra challenge by...

...encouraging more able students to write the first paragraph of the news story, describing the events of the case in exciting and emotive detail.

Big answer plenary	Ask students to reconsider the Big Question: *What makes detectives exciting?* Ask students to evaluate how exciting they have found the Poirot cases they have looked at in the lesson. Support them in identifying the particular elements of the cases that students have found exciting. Encourage students to find out how *The Murder of Roger Ackroyd* concludes.

DETECTIVES 6

Do you have good detective skills?

Assessment objectives
AO6 Use vocabulary and sentence structures for clarity, purpose and effect, with accurate spelling and punctuation.
AO7 Demonstrate presentation skills.
AO9 Use spoken English effectively in speeches and presentations.

Controlled assessment
- Silver Step component 1
- Gold Step component 1

Differentiated learning outcomes
- **Entry Level 1 students** should spell simple phonetically plausible and high-frequency words accurately in their presentations.
- **Entry Level 2 students** should spell phonetically plausible and most high-frequency words with growing accuracy in their presentation.
- **Entry Level 3 students** should spell most words, including common polysyllabic words, accurately in their presentation.
- **GCSE-ready students** should spell words generally accurately, including polysyllabic words that conform to regular patterns in their presentation.

Resources
- **Worksheets**: 6.1, 6.2, 6.3
- **PPT 6**: Do you have detective skills?
- Access to ICT, if possible
- Individual whiteboards

Big question *Do you have good detective skills?* Ask students to explain the techniques they use for checking their own work for errors. Explore whether these have any similarities with the way a detective might look for clues.

Getting you thinking

Write the letters c, k, S, h, l, o, e, r on the board and ask students to rearrange the letters to find the first name of a famous detective.

Display Slide 1 from **PPT 6**. If students have not managed to rearrange the anagram so far, ask if this image helps them solve the problem. Ask students for words that they associate with the detective. Write these words on the board and tell students they will be tested on the spelling of these words later in the lesson.

> **Give extra support by...**
> ...providing less able students with **Worksheet 6.2** to use as a key word mat.
> ...showing students clips and images of Sherlock Holmes in the BBC series, using websites such as www.bbc.co.uk/programmes/b018ttws .
>
> **Give extra challenge by...**
> ...encouraging more able students to use polysyllabic words that do not conform to regular patterns to describe Sherlock.

Explore the skills

Read through the text on **Worksheet 6.1** with the class. Give students 5–10 minutes to go through the passage circling the correct spellings (EL1 students) or correcting the spelling mistakes (EL2/EL3 students).

Once they have finished, ask students to explain to each other what strategies they use to detect spelling mistakes and work out the correct spellings.

Ask students if the passage has revealed anything else about Sherlock Holmes. Add these ideas to the list on the board.

> **Give extra support** by...
> ...asking students to use dictionaries to find the correct spellings of the first three words and then to practise these spellings on the sheet.
>
> **Give extra challenge** by...
> ...asking students to act as coaches, showing less able students how to scan the text for errors and explaining the strategies they use to work out correct spellings.

Develop the skills

Display Slide 2 of **PPT 6**. Discuss the methods that Holmes used to solve his cases.

Ask students to plan a one-minute presentation about Sherlock Holmes and his methods, supported by three slides. Distribute **Worksheet 6.3** for students to scaffold/plan their responses. Students should try to use as many of the words describing Holmes that are on the board as possible. Allow students 10-15 minutes to create their slides, using PowerPoint if available, or A3 sheets of paper. Help students to write in full sentences as far as possible and to spell words correctly.

Give students five minutes to show their slides to a partner, allowing them to check the spelling on each other's slides.

> **Give extra support** by...
> ...allowing students to create one slide showing a spider diagram of key words, along the lines of Slide 2. Check that spellings are correct as they work.

Apply the skills

Encourage students to suggest briefly ways that a presentation can be successfully delivered.

Allow students five minutes to practise their presentations, focusing on incorporating the techniques that have just been suggested. Remove the words describing Holmes from the board.

Students deliver their presentations. At the end of each presentation, students should conceal their slides and then suggest one word that the rest of the class have to spell. The rest of the class have to write the word on their individual whiteboards, trying to spell it correctly.

> **Give extra support** by...
> ...allowing students who are not comfortable presenting in front of the class to deliver their presentation to a small group of students or to a familiar adult.
>
> **Give extra challenge** by...
> ...encouraging students to identify aspects of the text on **Worksheet 6.1** that suggested the aspects of Holmes's character they have highlighted in their presentation.

Big answer plenary	Ask students to reconsider the Big Question: *Do you have good detective skills?* Ask each student to suggest one strategy that they will use in future to spot errors in their work and one method they will use to work out how to spell a word.

EXHIBITIONS 1

What is an exhibition?

Assessment objectives
AO1 Read and understand a range of texts: identify and interpret explicit and implicit information and ideas.
AO9 Use spoken English effectively in speeches and presentations.

Non-exam assessment
- Silver Step component 1
- Gold Step component 1

Differentiated learning outcomes
- **Entry Level 1 students** should locate some points and information in simple texts about exhibitions.
- **Entry Level 2 students** should locate main points and information in texts about exhibitions.
- **Entry Level 3 students** should locate key points in texts about exhibitions.
- **GCSE-ready students** should locate and use ideas and information in texts about exhibitions.

Resources
- **Worksheets**: 1.1, 1.2
- **PPT 1**: What is an exhibition?

Big question *What is an exhibition?* Ask students if they have been to an exhibition, prompting with specific questions as necessary. If they have, explore where they went and what the exhibition was about. Ask students to describe the experience, what they saw, what they did, whether they bought anything. If some students have been to the same exhibition, ask them to compare their views. For students who haven't been to an exhibition, ask what they might like to see an exhibition about.

Getting you thinking

Display Slide 1 from **PPT 1**. Explain to students that they are going to find out about different types of exhibitions: that exhibitions can be for historical things such as dinosaurs, new technology such as phones and computers, or for products in different industries, such as toys and games. Tell students they are going to watch a clip about the Natural History Museum to give them an example of an exhibition that is both exciting and educational. The clip can be accessed via the link on Slide 1.

After the clip discuss with students what they saw, whether it was what they expected to see at an exhibition, and which part interested them most. Ask whether anyone has been to that exhibition and, if so, what things they remember seeing there.

Put students together who have been to the same type of exhibition, for example food, cars, technology, history. Ask them to write down on sticky notes, in a few words, three experiences they remember, such as: 'lots of people', 'big place', 'exciting', 'tiring'. Put these on the board or wall. Ask each group to describe their experiences to the rest of the class. If no one has been to an exhibition, play the clip again and ask them to write down three things that look exciting, scary, interesting, etc.

> **Give extra support** by…
> … asking students to discuss the experiences they remember, while you write key words on the board.
> …describing your own personal experience of an exhibition.
>
> **Give extra challenge** by…
> …suggesting students research a few details of an exhibition that is being held or going to be held in the local area.

Explore the skills

Display Slide 2 of **PPT 1**, which gives a definition of an exhibition, and read the text with the students. On a card give each student a well-known brand name, such as Apple, Sony, Top Shop, Nike, Argos, PC World, and ask them to say, or write down on the card, what that company would show at an exhibition. Go round the class for answers.

> **Give extra support** by…
> … explaining that an exhibition is where companies can show their products to get people interested in buying them. Liken it to everyone having a shop in the same place. If students cannot grasp the concept, compare it to a car boot sale but on a far grander scale.
>
> **Give extra challenge** by…
> … putting the name of different products from these companies on card and asking students to match products to names.

Remind students that exhibitions can also be held for educational interest or fun reasons. Explain that a student called Anna has been on a school trip to a toys and games exhibition in London.

Ask students to read **Worksheet 1.1** and highlight any words they do not understand and need to have clarified. Go round and check students' understanding.

> **Give extra support** by…
> … asking students to think about what they might see at a toys and games exhibition, for example a hoverboard, computer games, new Lego.

Develop the skills

Distribute **Worksheet 1.2**, which works in conjunction with **Worksheet 1.1**. Allow students 5-10 minutes to complete the tasks, and then check answers.

Apply the skills

Display Slide 3 of **PPT 1**. Check that students are familiar with all the types of place shown in the picture. Ask for examples of a museum (e.g. Victoria and Albert), an exhibition centre (e.g. the National Exhibition Centre or NEC) and a palace (e.g. Buckingham Palace).

Ask students to work in small mixed-ability groups. Give each group three types of venue, taken from the slide, and ask them to suggest what sorts of exhibition might be held there and what types of objects they might see at each one. Each group can then feed their ideas back to the class.

> **Give extra support** by…
> … giving students a list of possible exhibition types to choose from.
>
> **Give extra challenge** by…
> … ask students to go on the internet and find actual venues for the three types of place on their card. A useful website is: www.venues.org.uk/exhibitions

Big answer plenary	Ask students to reconsider the Big Question: *What is an exhibition?* Ask them to think about what type of exhibition they would be interested in visiting, having learnt more about the different types. For students working at lower levels, suggest they answer with 'I would like to visit… because…'.

EXHIBITIONS 2

The Ideal Home Show

Assessment objectives

AO1 Read and understand a range of texts: identify and interpret explicit and implicit information and ideas.

Non-exam assessment
- Silver Step component 1
- Gold Step component 1

Differentiated learning outcomes
- **Entry Level 1 students** should recall main points from a simple text about a trip to the Ideal Home Show.
- **Entry Level 2 students** should recall some specific and straightforward information from a text about a trip to the Ideal Home Show.
- **Entry Level 3 students** should demonstrate an understanding of the main points in a text about a trip to the Ideal Home Show.
- **GCSE-ready students** should demonstrate a firm understanding of significant points in a text about a trip to the Ideal Home Show.

Resources
- **Worksheets**: 2.1, 2.2
- **PPT 2**: The Ideal Home Show

Big question — *What is the Ideal Home Show?* Ask students whether they have heard of this exhibition before and what they think they might see there. Give a hint that it is about things in a flat or house. Given what they learnt about exhibitions from Lesson 1, what sort of companies do they think might exhibit there? What sort of people do they think would be interested in going there?

Getting you thinking

Display Slide 1 from **PPT 2**: What is the Ideal Home Show? Click on the link to show students what it is about. Ask students to think of three things that stood out for them. Write each one on the board and see if there were any that most people remembered. Ask students why they think these stood out.

Recap from the previous lesson that many exhibitions only showcase one type of product (for example, toys or phones), but explain that the Ideal Home Show has hundreds of different products with something for all ages to see.

Give extra support by...
...discussing some of the things that were in the clip and then playing it again.

Give extra challenge by...
...asking students to make a list of everything they remember and to say what they thought was the most interesting thing and why.

Explore the skills

Explain to students that a visit to the Ideal Home Show needs to be planned, as it takes all day and is not free.

Ask students what they need to think about to plan a trip to the cinema, for example. Working in pairs, they should complete a spider diagram with all the things they need to think about, such as when to go, who to go with, what film to see, how to get there, what they will wear and how much money they will need. Give students ten minutes to discuss and write their notes.

Display Slide 2 from **PPT 2** and ask students if they have the same points. Do they have any additional points?

> **Give extra support** by...
>
> ...prompting some of the things they need to think about or referring them back to the last time they visited the cinema, a concert, etc., and asking what they needed to plan.
>
> **Give extra challenge** by...
>
> ...asking students, still in their pairs, to write down the points on their spider diagram as a list, in the order they think they should consider them – for example, what to see, when to go, etc.

Develop the skills

Distribute **Worksheets 2.1** and **2.2**. **Worksheet 2.1** describes a trip to the Ideal Home Show, with **Worksheet 2.2** providing tasks based on the text. Ask students to highlight any words they do not understand. Explain the meaning of these words within the context of the text. Allow students 5–10 minutes to complete the tasks.

> **Give extra support** by...
>
> ...reading the text with students.
>
> ...relating the text to what students saw on the YouTube clip – for example, the house, garden and food.
>
> **Give extra challenge** by...
>
> ...asking students working at a higher level to highlight linking words in the text ('and', 'but', 'so', etc.).

Apply the skills

Ask students to tell you what they need to think about if they are going to visit the Ideal Home Show. Write these on the board. If possible, allow students in pairs to visit the Ideal Home Show website (www.idealhomeshow.co.uk) and to work out which day would be the best for them to plan a visit there and how much it would cost for one adult and two Under-16s on that day.

Explain to students that when you visit such a large exhibition, it is a good idea to plan what you want to see and perhaps the order in which you want to go and look at things. Again using the Ideal Home Show website, ask them in their pairs to choose the areas of the Show they would be most interested in seeing, in order to plan their day.

Display Slide 3 from **PPT 2** as a prompt or, if it is not possible for students to access the Ideal Home website, use the slide as the basis for students to plan their day by asking them to put the things to see in their order of preference.

Ask more confident pairs to feed back to the class about the day they have planned.

> **Give extra challenge** by...
>
> ...asking other students to question their peers about the day they have planned, so that they need to justify their decisions.

| **Big answer plenary** | *What is the Ideal Home Show?* Students should be able to give examples of what the show is about, what they can see there, what they would prefer to see and why they need to plan any visit to such a big exhibition. |

EXHIBITIONS 3

The history of exhibitions

Assessment objectives

AO1 Read and understand a range of texts: identify and interpret explicit and implicit information and ideas.

Non-exam assessment
- Silver Step component 1
- Gold Step component 1

Differentiated learning outcomes
- **Entry Level 1 students** should read some high-frequency and familiar words in simple texts about the Great Exhibition.
- **Entry Level 2 students** should read with some fluency and accuracy texts including high-frequency, some medium-frequency and CVCC, CCVC words about the Great Exhibition.
- **Entry Level 3 students** should read fluently and accurately texts about the Great Exhibition.
- **GCSE-ready students** should read and understand a range of texts about the Great Exhibition.

Resources
- **Worksheets**: 3.1, 3.2
- **PPT 3**: Why do we go to exhibitions?

Big question *Why do we go to exhibitions?* Now that students have learnt more about what an exhibition is, and have looked at some examples, ask them why people may want to organise exhibitions and why other people may want to visit them. Ask students to suggest as many reasons as they can and write these in the form of a mind map.

Getting you thinking

Display Slide 1 of **PPT 3**. Explain to students that Queen Victoria and Prince Albert came up with the idea for the first large exhibition, as a way of showcasing Britain to the British people and to the rest of the world. Other countries were invited to exhibit there too. This was the Great Exhibition of 1851. Students may have heard of the Crystal Palace (from football if nothing else!); this was the huge glass palace built to house the Exhibition. Explain that it was built in Hyde Park in the centre of London and then moved to another park in South London after the close of the Exhibition.

Click on the first link to the Great Exhibition of 1851. Ask students for their first impressions about the Exhibition. Can they recall three things they saw in the video that were on display at the Exhibition? What would they have been particularly interested to see? Why do they think it was so popular?

Explore the skills

Distribute **Worksheet 3.1**. Ask students to read the text. Check understanding by asking them to highlight any words they do not know. When you are sure all students understand the text, they can go on to answer the questions.

> **Give extra support by…**
> …reading the text with the students.
> …explaining that the answers are highlighted and the students need to match them to the questions.
>
> **Give extra challenge by…**
> …showing the second clip about the exhibition and then asking students why they think Queen Victoria wanted to show these things about Great Britain: www.vam.ac.uk/content/videos/a/video-day-at-the-great-exhibition. The video is long, but can be stopped after 4.20 minutes if necessary.

Develop the skills

Remind students from previous lessons that an exhibition is a good way to let people see objects such as art, textiles, and treasures from many years ago, but that today there are many reasons why people have exhibitions. As well as large exhibitions in cities, there can also be very small exhibitions in local libraries or community centres.

Display Slide 2 from **PPT 3**. Discuss with students the different reasons shown on the slide why people go to exhibitions today. Ask students as a group to suggest an example against each reason shown: for example, to learn – Science Museum; to admire – buried treasure; to have fun – Alice in Wonderland exhibition; to buy – Harry Potter memorabilia at a toy fair; to make choices – new phone, new school, etc.

> **Give extra support** by...
> ...giving examples, by referring to the Natural History Museum and the Ideal Home Show as large exhibitions in cities, in contrast to a school, library or community centre exhibition in their local area, which might have paintings by local artists or a project on local history by schoolchildren.
>
> **Give extra challenge** by...
> ...encouraging students also to think of reasons why people might want to hold an exhibition. (The later part of the video about the Great Exhibition gives another possible reason: the money made from the Great Exhibition was used to build the Science, Natural History and Victoria and Albert Museums in London.).

Apply the skills

Display Slide 3 from **PPT 3**. Distribute **Worksheet 3.2**, which asks students to choose which exhibition out of the four listed they would like to go to.

Ask the students to think about why they have put the types of exhibitions in the order they have and why they have selected a particular exhibition as their first choice.

> **Give extra support** by...
> ...suggesting what students could see and do at each of the four exhibitions.
>
> **Give extra challenge** by...
> ...asking students to research on the internet where they might find their first choice of exhibition.

Ask more-confident students to give a brief explanation to the rest of the class about why they made their first choice. They can ask for the PPT slides to be played again or put up on the screen. Encourage other students in the class to question them or challenge their choice.

> **Give extra support** by...
> ...giving a model for their presentation/speech. For example, 'I would like to go to an exhibition about... because...'.

Big answer plenary	*Why do we go to exhibitions?* Ask students to think about the Great Exhibition again and why it was so popular. A further exhibition – the Festival of Britain – was held 100 years later, in 1951, and also proved very popular. Much of the exhibition looked to the future and new inventions. Do students think a similar exhibition planned now would be successful?

EXHIBITIONS 4

Famous museums

Assessment objectives

AO5 Communicate clearly, effectively and imaginatively, selecting and adapting tone, style and register for different forms, purposes and audiences.

AO6 Use vocabulary and sentence structures for clarity, purpose and effect, with accurate spelling and punctuation.

Non-exam assessment
- Silver Step component 1
- Gold Step component 1

Differentiated learning outcomes
- **Entry Level 1 students** should use some simple descriptive language when designing a leaflet for a museum.
- **Entry Level 2 students** should use appropriate words to create interest when designing a leaflet for a museum.
- **Entry Level 3 students** should choose words for variety and interest when writing an email about a trip to a museum.
- **GCSE-ready students** should make adventurous and effective choice of vocabulary when writing an email about a trip to a museum.

Resources
- **Worksheets**: 4.1, 4.2
- **PPT 4**: Famous museums

Big question — *What are museums?* Ask students whether they have been to a museum. Suggest a few famous museums that they may have visited, such as the Victoria and Albert Museum, the Natural History Museum, the Imperial War Museums, the Science Museum and the National Railway Museum. If any students have visited a museum, ask them to say which one, so that you can write the name on the board.

Getting you thinking

Display Slide 1 of **PPT 4** and show the clip about the National Railway Museum. Ask students what they liked or didn't like about the museum, e.g. fun things to do, can go as a family, can see old trains, may be more suited to young children.

Show the clip again and ask students why they think it is called a museum and not an exhibition. Compare it with the Ideal Home Show and tease out answers by asking if the Railway Museum is only there for a short period or if it is open all year round.

Explore the skills

Distribute **Worksheet 4.1**. For EL1 & EL2 students, explain that they need to read the text about Robbie's visit to the National Railway Museum, correct the punctuation errors, capital letters and full stops, and then design a leaflet for the Museum.

EL3-level students should work in small groups to correct the punctuation errors and then plan an email to their head teacher trying to persuade them to organise a school trip to the National Railway Museum. They should base their email on the content of the poster they have read, to say why they would like to go and what they would like to see. Write the following on the board to support them if necessary:

We would really like it if you could organise a class trip to the National Railway Museum. It looks really good because... You can see...

If there is access to Wi-Fi, tell students to send a final draft to their tutor.

> **Give extra support by...**
> ...reminding students as appropriate that a sentence starts with a capital letter and ends in a full stop, that proper nouns (names) have a capital letter and that 'I' should always be a capital letter.

Give extra challenge by...

...asking students to go on the internet to find the top three major museums in the UK, write these down and say how many visitors they get each year. A useful website is: https://en.wikipedia.org/wiki/List_of_most_visited_museums_in_the_United_Kingdom

Develop the skills

Display Slide 2 from **PPT 4**. Put students into three groups. On a piece of paper give each group a name – British Museum, Victoria and Albert Museum or Science Museum. If students have access to the internet, ask them to research two facts about 'their' museum (www.visitbritain.com/en/Things-to-do/Culture/Free-museums.html). Groups then share their findings with the class. (If internet access is not available, print out sheets from the sites for students to use.)

Now distribute **Worksheet 4.2**. Check understanding of the text by asking questions, such as:

- Where can you see old treasure?
- Where can you find wigs and hats?
- In which museum can you look at bugs?

Discuss with students the reasons why they might like to go to a certain museum, in preparation for completing the rest of **Worksheet 4.2**.

Allow 10 minutes for students to complete the tasks and then ask more confident students to say which exhibition they would like to go to and why. Ask them to share their sentences to make each exhibition sound like fun. Remind them that adjectives ('amazing', 'spine-chilling') and superlatives ('greatest', 'biggest') can help with this.

Apply the skills

Tell students that they are going to research a museum of their choice. They may have their own ideas or can do research into a museum in the local area. Alternatively, show Slide 3 of **PPT 4**, which lists some unusual museums that might appeal!

Display Slide 4 of **PPT 4**. Explain that a slogan is a short sentence summing up why the museum is so good. Tell students they need to write a slogan that makes their chosen museum sound interesting to persuade people to come and visit. Draw attention to the use of adjectives ('leading') and superlatives ('greatest') in the examples, and suggest students should include one in their own slogan.

Ask more confident students to read out their slogan to the class. Do other students think the museum sounds a good place to visit?

Give extra support by...

...giving examples of familiar slogans for well-known brands, e.g. 'Finger lickin' good' (KFC), 'I'm lovin' it' (MacDonalds) or 'Just do it' (Nike). Ask students what these slogans suggest about the product or brand and why they are so memorable.

Give extra challenge by...

...telling GCSE-ready students to write a short blurb on the museum of their choice; encourage them to have a clear idea in mind of who their target audience is and to use the appropriate language.

Big answer plenary	*What are museums?* Ask students what they now understand museums to be: that is, places where objects of interest are stored and displayed, as opposed to exhibitions that can only be seen for a few days or weeks. From all the museums the students have looked at, which would they most like to visit?

EXHIBITIONS 5

An exhibition near you

Assessment objectives

AO5 Communicate clearly, effectively and imaginatively, selecting and adapting tone, style and register for different forms, purposes and audiences.

AO6 Use vocabulary and sentence structures for clarity, purpose and effect, with accurate spelling and punctuation.

Non-exam assessment
- Silver Step component 1
- Gold Step component 1

Differentiated learning outcomes
- **Entry Level 1 students** should use some simple descriptive language when writing about objects to include in a capsule.
- **Entry Level 2 students** should use appropriate words to create interest when writing about objects to include in a capsule.
- **Entry Level 3 students** should choose words for variety and interest when writing about objects to include in a capsule.
- **GCSE-ready students** should make adventurous and effective choice of vocabulary when writing about objects to include in a capsule.

Resources
- **Worksheets**: 5.1, 5.2
- **PPT 5**: An exhibition near you
- A mock 'time capsule' containing objects such as clothes, money, canned foods, photographs, documents, a smartphone

Big question — *What type of exhibitions are there in your area?* Remind students that exhibitions and museums are not just in large cities. Do they know of anything happening in local schools, libraries, community centres or even outdoors in town centres? How much do they know about the history of their area? Or of their school?

Getting you thinking

Display Slide 1 from **PPT 5**. Explain to students that many towns have local exhibitions and museums that focus on history and past events in that area. Click on the link about Leicester Museums and play the video right through. Discuss with students what they can recall from it. Does anyone know what 'medieval' means? Explain that it is the time between the 5th and 15th centuries.

Play the video again and ask students to choose one part that particularly appeals to them. Stop the video at intervals to check students are aware of what is being shown and what the key events are, such as the arrival of the Black Death and the Battle of Bosworth. Ask some students to say which part interests them and to explain why. Then ask all students to write a phrase or sentence to say which part interests them and why. Remind students to use correct punctuation (capital letters and full stops).

> **Give extra support by...**
> ...writing an example on the board as your answer, e.g. 'I would like to know more the Black Death. It looks grim.'
>
> **Give extra challenge by...**
> ...asking students to find out one (or more) other facts about Leicester and its history. They can research on www.visitleicester.info/things-to-see-and-do .

Explore the skills

Tell students that they are now going to find out about another sort of local museum that shows more recent history. Point out that even their own childhoods are now part of history! Distribute **Worksheet 5.1**, which is about the museum of children's television in Portsmouth. Make sure all students are clear about the instructions.

When students have completed the task and you have checked answers, discuss with students the television characters they can remember from their childhood. Who did they like watching, and why? For EL1 and EL2 students, ask them to write a phrase or simple sentence about the character; some students at these levels could try to extend the sentence. Ask EL3 students to write about two characters and say which character they preferred. Tell Silver level students to start their sentence with 'xxx is my favourite character because …'

Give extra support by…
…giving examples of characters and asking specific questions about them – for example, were they good, bad, funny, helpful, etc.

Give extra challenge by…
…asking students to write a sentence describing each character. For an even greater challenge, ask them to identify the adjectives in their sentences.

Develop the skills

Display Slide 2 from **PPT 5**. Ask students what a 'time capsule' is. If no one knows, ask them to speculate about what it might be. Explain that it is a box with information and objects in it that will tell people in the future how we lived today – rather like setting up an exhibition about the present for people to see in the future. They are usually buried underground for someone to find in 100 years or more.

Discuss the type of things that might go into a time capsule, such as clothes, money, canned foods, photographs, documents or technology such as smartphones. You may find it useful to bring in a time capsule that you have already prepared before the lesson with some of these objects inside. What other ideas can students come up with that really sum up life today? Explain to students that a time capsule often contains a note from the person who buried it that describes what life at that time was like.

Give extra challenge by…
…asking students to find out, using the internet, whether any time capsules have been found or been buried in their area.

Apply the skills

Tell students they are going to write about objects to put in a time capsule for someone who might find it in 100 years. The objects can be about their life today, transport they use, clothes they wear, technology they use, food they eat.

Display Slide 3 from **PPT 5**. Explain to students that in their information they will want to use describing words, which are called adjectives, and action words, which are called verbs. Talk through the examples on the slide. Ask students to replace the adjectives and verbs in bold with another word. Then put students into pairs and ask them to put the words at the bottom of the slide into two columns, adjectives and verbs, then check answers. For EL1 & EL2 students, go through each word and ask what they think the word is and write it in two columns on the board.

Distribute **Worksheet 5.2** for students to write information about their time capsule. Ask more confident students to read out their descriptions and to compare what they put in their capsules.

Give extra support by…
…recapping what sorts of things can be put in a time capsule.

Big answer plenary	*What type of exhibitions are there in your area?* Ask students if they now feel more aware of the type of exhibitions and museums that may be in the local area. Ask them again what these might be. Ask students to suggest a local exhibition they would like to see. Ask if they can suggest where they might bury a time capsule.

EXHIBITIONS 6: Planning an exhibition

Assessment objectives
AO5 Communicate clearly, effectively and imaginatively, selecting and adapting tone, style and register for different forms, purposes and audiences.

AO8 Listen and respond appropriately to spoken language, including to questions and feedback on presentations.

Non-exam assessment
- Silver Step component 1
- Gold Step component 1

Differentiated learning outcomes
- **Entry Level 1 students** should engage with others.
- **Entry Level 2 students** should engage with others, making simple comments and suggestions.
- **Entry Level 3 students** should respond to others, developing ideas and making helpful comments and suggestions.
- **GCSE-ready students** should make contributions and ask questions that are responsive to others' views and ideas.

Resources
- **Worksheets**: 6.1
- **PPT 6**: Planning an exhibition

Big question — *How do you plan an exhibition?* Ask students if they have been involved in planning or helping to plan an exhibition, maybe at primary school. If they have, ask them to tell the group what they had to do, what type of exhibition it was and who it was for.

Getting you thinking

Display Slide 1 from **PPT 6**. Explain to students that one of the best ways to know what is involved in an exhibition is to plan one. Tell students they are going to watch a video clip of an exhibition that a primary school arranged. Play a brief section of the clip and ask students what type of exhibition it was, i.e. arts and crafts. Ask what types of things were in the exhibition (pictures, models, pretty boxes, jewellery, etc.).

Tell students that this lesson will be about them planning an exhibition at their school. It will involve working in groups, with students deciding who does what job and what needs to be done to make it successful. The students will need to listen to each other, ask each other questions and then agree on everything that needs to be done.

Put students into small groups of mixed ability to brainstorm what type of exhibition they would like to plan and the reason they have chosen this exhibition.

Give extra support by...
...pointing out the types of things that could be in their exhibition.

Give extra challenge by...
...asking students to make a list of the items (exhibits) that were shown in the video; this might help them later in their planning.

Explore the skills

Display Slide 2 from **PPT 6**. Put students into groups of four or five and distribute **Worksheet 6.1**. Explain to students that this is their planning sheet for the exhibition. In their groups, they need to agree on what they are going to do in more detail. They can refer to the slide to help fill in the boxes. Allow 10–15 minutes for this.

Ask each group to feed back to the class about their plans. Encourage other students to ask questions and challenge. Discuss with students the importance of listening to the speaker, taking turns to respond and putting their hands up to ask a question. Explain that when they are speaking to the class, they should make eye contact, speak clearly and look enthusiastic. This is an opportunity to demonstrate some of the things not to do, such as looking at the ceiling when they talk, mumbling or sounding miserable! Explain the importance of non-verbal, or body, language and ask them to display some examples of non-verbal language, such as a smiling face, unhappy face, arms crossed as if bored or annoyed, rolling their eyes as if annoyed.

> **Give extra support** by…
> …referring students to Slide 2 to help with completing **Worksheet 6.1**.
> …asking questions and challenging groups yourself, to give a lead.

Develop the skills

Tell the groups that they have to go through their plan and decide on each person's role, i.e. who is going to do what job(s). Remind students to listen to each other's views, ask questions respectfully, help to develop ideas and learn how to work with others, even if they don't always agree.

Tell each group to produce a list of things that need to be done (ask a more confident student to act as scribe) and against each task indicate who is doing what.

> **Give extra support** by…
> …suggesting roles, e.g. administration – involves finding out when the room is free and booking a time.
>
> **Give extra challenge** by…
> …asking the name of roles people can take, e.g. chair, publicity, secretary, and what those roles entail.

Apply the skills

Explain to students that now that they have organised what they are doing, they need to promote the exhibition by producing an invitation and a poster for the event. Check understanding of the word 'promote' and remind students of some of the promotional material they have seen about museums and exhibitions in earlier lessons.

Display Slide 3 from **PPT 6**, which includes some suggestions for what students need to include on their invitations. Now ask students to design their invitation using ICT. Work with students to show the order in which the information needs to appear.

Ask students from each group to present their invitations to the class and tell them they are going to vote for which one is best. Remind students that when they present their work, they need to look at their audience, look and sound positive and speak clearly. The rest of the class should offer helpful suggestions and comments during the presentations.

> **Give extra support** by…
> …suggesting words for the invitation to attract people to the exhibition, such as great, interesting, pretty, new, etc.
>
> **Give extra challenge** by…
> …asking students to prepare a ticket suitable either for other students at school, or for teachers and parents. Will the ticket be different depending on who will see it?
> …asking students to design a poster for the exhibition.

Big answer plenary	*How do you plan an exhibition?* Ask students to reconsider the question. What have they learnt about this from the lesson? Is it easier or harder than they expected?

TRAVEL 1

Where to go on holiday?

Assessment objectives
AO1 Read and understand a range of texts: identify and interpret explicit and implicit information and ideas.

Non-exam assessment
- Silver Step component 1
- Gold Step component 1

Differentiated learning outcomes
- **Entry Level 1 students** should locate some points and information in a simple text about a travel destination.
- **Entry Level 2 students** should locate main points and information in a text about a travel destination.
- **Entry Level 3 students** should locate key points in a text about travel destinations.
- **GCSE-ready students** should locate and use ideas and information about travel destinations.

Resources
- **Worksheets**: 1.1, 1.2
- **PPT 1**: How do people choose where to go on holiday?

Big question — *How do people choose where to go on holiday?* Discuss with students any holidays that they have been on. Ask them what they enjoyed about these holidays and whether there are any destinations they would like to revisit. If so, encourage them to explain their reasons for liking the destination so much.

Getting you thinking

Display Slide 1 of **PPT 1**. Ask students to write down any words that come to mind when they look at the images on the screen. Share the words with the class.

Introduce the words 'destination' and 'tourist' and check that the class know what they mean. In pairs, allow students 2–3 minutes to discuss what the appeal of each destination might be to a potential tourist. Instruct students to write two short phrases (EL1) / simple sentences (EL2) / extended sentences (EL3 & GCSE-ready) about the images, explaining which destinations they would most and least like to visit and why.

> **Give extra support** by…
> …encouraging students to suggest which image most closely resembles a holiday that they have been on and to explain the similarities.
>
> **Give extra challenge** by…
> …asking students to explain what their perfect holiday would be, combining elements from as many of the images as possible.

Explore the skills

Display Slide 2 of **PPT 1** and distribute individual whiteboards to students. As a class, read the survey results from the HolidayTips website. Ask the class each of the questions below in turn, allowing students 10 seconds to write the correct answer on their individual whiteboards. Ask students who answer a question correctly to explain which detail of the text led them to their response.

Q1 – What was the average rating people gave to the food in Newquay? (5.4)
Q2 – Which destination was the most popular overall? (Edinburgh)
Q3 – What was one of the problems faced by visitors to the Lake District? (rain)
Q4 – According to the comments, which destination has nice beaches? (Jersey)

Give extra support by…

…allowing students to work in small groups, sharing one whiteboard between them. Allow the students extra time to discuss their answers before writing them on the whiteboards.

Give extra challenge by…

…encouraging students to write their answers in full sentences, using 'because' to explain how they arrived at their conclusion.

Develop the skills

Distribute **Worksheet 1.1**. Read through the holiday brochure description and check that the class has understood the text.

Allow students 5–10 minutes to answer the questions on the worksheet by recognising short phrases (EL1), or using simple sentences (EL2) or extended sentences (EL3 & GCSE-ready).

In pairs, students should compare their answers, explain to each other which details of the brochure description they used to answer each question and discuss any disagreements.

Give extra support by…

…supplying the line numbers for the key pieces of information that students will need to complete each question.

Give extra challenge by…

…encouraging students to use direct quotations from the brochure description to support their answers.

Apply the skills

Display Slide 3 of **PPT 1**. Tell students that they are going to pretend to be travel agents and that they must recommend where the three customers shown on the slide should go on holiday.

Distribute **Worksheet 1.2**. Read through the holiday descriptions and check that the class understands the texts. Give students 10 minutes to write down their holiday recommendations for each customer. They should provide at least two reasons why they feel each customer would enjoy a particular holiday destination.

Give extra support by…

…asking students to pick out the attractions of each destination, rather than tailoring their recommendations to particular customers.

Give extra challenge by…

…encouraging students to respond in role, trying to make their recommendations as persuasive as possible and including some advice to the would-be travellers about how to get the most out of their holiday destination.

Big answer plenary	Ask students to reconsider the Big Question: *How do people choose where to go on holiday?* As students leave the room, ask each one for one piece of advice they would give to people looking to go on holiday about how to choose the best possible destination.

TRAVEL 2
What would you tell people about your holiday?

Assessment objectives

AO1 Read and understand a range of texts: identify and interpret explicit and implicit information and ideas.

AO5 Communicate clearly, effectively and imaginatively, selecting and adapting tone, style and register for different forms, purposes and audiences.

Non-exam assessment
- Silver Step component 1
- Gold Step component 1

Differentiated learning outcomes
- **Entry Level 1 students** should sometimes arrange details of a holiday in an appropriate order.
- **Entry Level 2 students** should describe a holiday mainly in simple sequenced sentences.
- **Entry Level 3 students** should sequence details of a holiday logically in sentences that are usually grammatically correct.
- **GCSE-ready students** should sequence details of a holiday in a sustained, developed and interesting way.

Resources
- **Worksheets**: 2.1, 2.2, 2.3
- **PPT 2**: What would you tell people about your holiday?

Big question | *What would you tell people about your holiday?* Ask students to come up with as many words as they can to describe a holiday. Prompt them to think of descriptions for different aspects of a holiday: accommodation, weather, food, activities, etc.

Getting you thinking

Display Slide 1 of **PPT 2**. For EL1 & EL2, put each of the following words on a piece of card and distribute to the class: good, bad, tall, deep, rain, sad, tasty, nice.

Read the sentences on the postcard one at a time and ask students to hold up an appropriate word to fill in the gap. For EL3 & GCSE-ready students, check that the class understands the text; then put students into groups of three or four and allow them 3–5 minutes to suggest suitable words to fill in the gaps in the postcard.

Share groups' ideas with the rest of the class and discuss how different groups' choices alter the tone of the message. Encourage students to suggest how the tone should be altered for different potential audiences, e.g. an elderly relative, your best friend, a young niece or nephew.

Give extra support by…
…suggesting words that could fill the gaps and asking students to suggest synonyms that would maintain the sense of the message.

Give extra challenge by…
…challenging students to select words that imply their holiday was a negative experience while not saying so explicitly.

Explore the skills

Distribute **Worksheet 2.1** to the class. Read the text as a class and check that students understand the text.

Ask students to answer the comprehension questions on the worksheet, working individually. Allow approximately 5 minutes for this task.

> **Give extra support by…**
> …providing students with the line or paragraph numbers of key pieces of information to help them answer the questions.
>
> **Give extra challenge by…**
> …encouraging students to refer to specific textual details in their answers.

Develop the skills

Display Slide 2 of **PPT 2**. Tell students that they are going to imagine they are Calla and that they are going to write a letter to her grandmother describing the problems with her holiday.

Using **Worksheet 2.2**, students can plan out which details they would include in their letter.

> **Give extra support by…**
> …re-reading **Worksheet 2.1** with students to remind them of what happened to Calla.
>
> **Give extra challenge by…**
> …challenging students to use understatement when describing the issues they've faced, so as not to worry their grandmother.

Apply the skills

Display Slide 3 of **PPT 2**. Still in role as Calla, students should write their letter to their grandmother. Students should use **Worksheet 2.3** as a structure.

Students get into pairs (EL1 students should pair up with a trusted adult) and read each other's work. They then give their partner two pieces of positive feedback about their work and one suggestion for how to improve it further.

> **Give extra support by…**
> …allowing students to copy appropriate words and phrases from **Worksheet 2.2**.
>
> **Give extra challenge by…**
> …encouraging more confident students to invent further issues with Calla's holiday beyond those mentioned to her friend and incorporate these into their responses.

Big answer plenary	Ask students to reconsider the Big Question: *What would you tell people about your holiday?* In pairs, students should discuss what details of their holidays they would relate to a range of different audiences, and the kind of language they would use to express these details. You could support their discussion by asking students to think of things that they might tell different people: i.e. parents, friends, a best friend or a teacher. What things would they *not* tell certain people? For example, they might not tell their mum and dad they had done something dangerous such as paragliding or that they had met an attractive boy/girl on holiday, whereas they would tell their best friend. They might tell their teacher about how they had spoken Spanish on holiday, but may not tell their friend this as they wouldn't be interested. In the whole group, ask for examples of things they would / would not tell different people.

TRAVEL 3

Holidays in the 19th century

Assessment objectives

AO1 Read and understand a range of texts: identify and interpret explicit and implicit information and ideas.

AO8 Listen and respond appropriately to spoken language, including to questions and feedback on presentations.

Non-exam assessment

- Silver Step component 1
- Gold Step component 1

Differentiated learning outcomes

- **Entry Level 1 students** should locate some points and information in simple texts about the seaside in the 19th century.
- **Entry Level 2 students** should locate main points and information in texts about the seaside in the 19th century.
- **Entry Level 3 students** should locate key points in texts about the seaside in the 19th century.
- **GCSE-ready students** should locate and use ideas and information in texts about the seaside in the 19th century.

Resources

- **Worksheets**: 3.1, 3.2
- **PPT 3**: Where did people go on holiday in the 19th century?
- Dictionaries

Big question *Where did people go on holiday in the 19th century?* Discuss with students what they know about Victorian Britain. Ask them to make guesses about what kinds of holidays people might have enjoyed during the period.

Getting you thinking

Display Slide 1 of **PPT 3**. Ask students to suggest words or phrases that come to their mind when they look at the images. Record students' thoughts on the board.

Explain that these images show Blackpool, which is still a popular destination today. Ask each student to write down two things that might attract tourists to Blackpool, in full sentences if possible.

Give extra support by…
…beginning the task with a whole-class discussion of what the images show before asking students to write down their own ideas.

Give extra challenge by…
…asking students to evaluate the extent to which they feel the images of Blackpool portray it as an attractive destination for tourists in the 21st century.

Explore the skills

Display Slide 2 of **PPT 3**. Explain to students that this image shows Blackpool beach in the Victorian era. Ask students to use **Worksheet 3.1** to note down any holiday activities they can see in the picture. Ask students whether the things they have spotted are the same as or different from Blackpool today.

Play students this clip: www.youtube.com/watch?v=rwoU_Rk4m-o

Students should add any extra information they have learnt about Victorian Blackpool to their sheets.

> **Give extra support** by...
> ... listing on the board some CVCC/CCVC words that EL1 students may need to access the task
> ...helping students to explain verbally the similarities and differences between holidays in Blackpool then and now, using the details from **Worksheet 3.1**.

Develop the skills

Display Slide 3 of **PPT 3** and distribute **Worksheet 3.2**. Give students a few minutes to read through the text of Molly's visit to Blackpool and ask the meanings of any unfamiliar words.

Ask students to explain what Molly did when she was in Blackpool.

> **Give extra support** by...
> ...writing on the board activities Molly might have done and asking students to say whether she did them or not.
>
> **Give extra challenge** by...
> ...asking students to imagine they are Molly explaining what she did in Blackpool and encouraging them to bring out her thoughts and feelings about the trip.

Apply the skills

Ask students to complete the tasks on **Worksheet 3.2**. Through questioning of the class, establish whether they feel Molly enjoyed her day in Blackpool.

Students should try to complete the statement: 'Molly enjoyed her day in Blackpool because...' EL1 students will use a simple phrase, while EL2 students should complete the sentence. EL3 and GCSE-ready students should write a short paragraph using specific details.

Ask students to look back through their work and underline any points where they have referred to specific details of Molly's account. Encourage confident students to share their work with the rest of the class.

> **Give extra support** by...
> ...encouraging students to list aspects of her visit to Blackpool that Molly enjoyed and another list of aspects she didn't enjoy.
>
> **Give extra challenge** by...
> ...asking more able students to infer Molly's attitudes towards her visit to Blackpool, using direct quotations to support their arguments.

Big answer plenary	Ask students to reconsider the Big Question: *Where did people go on holiday in the 19th century?* In pairs, students should explain to each other what they have learnt about holidays in the Victorian era and in what ways they were similar to or different from the holidays that people enjoy today.

TRAVEL 4

Exciting holiday destinations

Assessment objectives

AO7 Demonstrate presentation skills.

AO9 Use spoken English effectively in speeches and presentations.

Non-exam assessment
- Silver Step component 1
- Gold Step component 1

Differentiated learning outcomes
- **Entry Level 1 students** should communicate feelings and ideas about a holiday destination.
- **Entry Level 2 students** should communicate experiences, thoughts and feelings, linking ideas about a holiday destination.
- **Entry Level 3 students** should make sustained contributions, developing ideas and feelings about a holiday destination, using adjectives to maintain interest.
- **GCSE-ready students** should adapt talk to purpose: developing ideas, describing events and conveying opinions about a holiday destination clearly and thoughtfully.

Resources
- **Worksheets**: 4.1, 4.2
- **PPT 4**: How do you make a holiday destination sound exciting?

Big question

How do you make a holiday destination sound exciting? Play students an advert for a theme park, such as the one shown here: www.youtube.com/watch?v=dzVnScotTts

Ask students to suggest how the advert encourages people to visit Thorpe Park. EL1 and EL2 students can focus on the visuals, while more confident students should focus on the language used.

Getting you thinking

Display image Slide 1 of **PPT 4**. Ask the students what details they can see in the image and which words they could use to describe them.

Pair students with trusted adults and put more confident students into groups. Ask students to use **Worksheet 4.1** to discuss with the rest of the group what they can see, trying where possible to use adjectives to make the scene sound exciting.

> **Give extra support** by...
> ...providing students with choices about what they can see (for example, 'Can you see sun or snow?').
>
> **Give extra challenge** by...
> ...encouraging students to describe the scene as if they were there experiencing it at first hand.

Explore the skills

Model putting the words into simple sentences and saying them out loud (for example, 'There is sand. The sky is blue'). Students should practise putting their own words into simple sentences and saying these sentences aloud to a partner.

Model for students how to ask each other how they feel about each detail (for example, 'How does the sun make you feel?') and how to answer these questions (for example, 'The sun makes me feel hot.') Encourage students to ask each other to explain how each detail would make them feel.

> **Give extra support** by...
> ...allowing students to question a familiar adult first, and then answer questions from a familiar adult.
>
> **Give extra challenge** by...
> ...encouraging students to include powerful adjectives and adverbs in their responses.

Develop the skills

Display Slide 2 of **PPT 4**. Discuss which types of holidays these pictures suggest. Ask students to explain whether they have been on any holidays similar to these or any other holidays that they particularly enjoyed. Ask students to use **Worksheet 4.2** to describe this holiday experience, or one of the holidays suggested by the slide, to their trusted adult or students in their group.

Display Slide 3 of **PPT 4**. Model speaking in front of a group of people, by describing a great holiday experience you had. Through questioning, establish the strategies you have used to engage your audience (i.e. eye contact, gesture, emphasising key words).

Ask students to work in pairs to practise describing their favourite holiday. They can continue to use **Worksheet 4.2**, if needed, as prompts and instructions. Encourage them to incorporate some of the techniques from your modelling into their presentations. If possible, the pairs should record their presentations using video, tablet or smart phones. By playing back the recording, they can see and hear clearly how well they come across and what they need to improve for their presentation.

> **Give extra support** by...
> ...allowing students to listen to a familiar adult presenting to them first; then support them in copying what they have heard.
>
> **Give extra challenge** by...
> ...encouraging students to move from the words written on their worksheets to more natural, spontaneous speech.

Apply the skills

Ask students to deliver their presentations either to a familiar adult, the rest of their class or students/staff from a different class as appropriate. While they are listening to other students giving presentations, ask students to note down positive and negative aspects of the presentations. Guide students to give this feedback, focusing on suggestions for improvements and ensuring the feedback is constructive. **Worksheet 4.3** can be used to support students in this, if appropriate.

Students should note down one way in which they would improve their own presentation if they were to repeat it in the future.

> **Give extra support** by...
> ...allowing students to say one thing they liked about their own presentation, rather than giving feedback to others.
>
> **Give extra challenge** by...
> ...encouraging students to respond to questions from their audience.

| **Big answer plenary** | Ask students to reconsider the Big Question: *How do you make a holiday destination sound exciting?* Ask students to come up with one word or technique that they have used in their presentation to make their destination sound exciting. |

TRAVEL 5

Holidays of the future

Assessment objectives
AO8 Listen and respond appropriately to spoken language, including to questions and feedback on presentations.

Non-exam assessment
- Silver Step component 1
- Gold Step component 1

Differentiated learning outcomes
- **Entry Level 1 students** should agree or disagree with a comment or idea about holidays in space.
- **Entry Level 2 students** should agree or disagree with an idea about holidays in space and sometimes suggest an alternative.
- **Entry Level 3 students** should make helpful comments and suggestions about what they have heard about holidays in space.
- **GCSE-ready students** should ask questions about people's views on holidays in space and give reasons for their own viewpoint.

Resources
- **Worksheets**: 5.1, 5.2
- **PPT 5**: Where will people go on holiday in the future?

Big question
Where will people go on holiday in the future? Ask students to consider their own responses to this question, then play them footage of someone in space, for example this footage of British astronaut Tim Peake:

www.independent.co.uk/news/science/tim-peake-british-astronaut-says-life-in-space-way-beyond-expectations-in-first-press-conference-a6778881.html

Ask students whether they would ever consider going on holiday in space.

Getting you thinking

Display Slide 1 of **PPT 5**. Through class Q&A, try to explore some of the positive and negative aspects of holidaying in space. What would be good or bad about a holiday in space? Write students' responses on the board, underlining key words.

Ask the class to vote on whether they feel they would enjoy a holiday in space or not. Record the results of the vote for use later in the lesson.

> **Give extra support** by...
> ...asking students to think what they enjoy about holidays on Earth and then help them to explore whether these factors would potentially be the same or different in space.
>
> **Give extra challenge** by...
> ...encouraging students to challenge each other's opinions and suggest reasons for their own opinions.

Explore the skills

Cut up **Worksheet 5.1** and give one of the ideas to each member of the class. Students have to stand up, read their statement and then arrange themselves across the room according to whether they think their statement suggests a positive or a negative aspect of holidays in space. Students standing by the left-hand wall think their statement is very positive, students in the middle think their statement is neither positive nor negative, while those by the right-hand wall think their statement is very negative.

Ask students to question each other as to why they have chosen to stand where they have. Encourage students to respond appropriately and in detail.

Give extra support by...

...allowing students to question trusted adults who have taken up positions in the room.

Give extra challenge by...

...encouraging more confident students to take on a role (e.g. a space tour promoter, a mother with young children) and present their statement from this perspective.

Develop the skills

Display Slide 2 of **PPT 5.2**. Explain the concept of arguing for or against a statement.

Partner students with either a trusted adult (EL1), a trusted peer (EL2) or a student of similar ability (EL3 & GCSE-ready). Designate each pairing as arguing either for or against the statement: 'Space would be a great place for a holiday.' Students should use **Worksheet 5.2** to plan their arguments together. Silver level students should choose three of the reasons and label them 1, 2, 3 in order of importance, where 1 = their main argument.

Encourage students to suggest one or more alternatives to the statements given on the worksheet that they can use in their arguments.

Give extra support by...

...giving an example phrase (EL1) or sentence (EL2) showing how students can use their chosen ideas. For example, for 'There are risks', they could say 'like risks – fun/exciting' to argue in favour of the statement; or they could put 'do not like risks – scary' to argue against it.

Give extra challenge by...

...encouraging students working at a higher level to conduct independent research into the development of space tourism, using sites such as www.virgingalactic.com.

Apply the skills

Display Slide 3 of **PPT 5**. Ask students to use the ideas from **Worksheet 5.2** to discuss whether space would be a good destination for a holiday.

Ask the class to vote again on whether they feel space would be a good holiday destination. Discuss with students whether the results of the vote have changed from earlier in the lesson and, if possible, ask students to justify why their views have changed or remained the same.

Give extra support by...

...allowing students to listen to a trusted adult discussing the topic. Students should indicate whether they agree or disagree with the ideas they hear.

Give extra challenge by...

...encouraging students to question each other's statements and to challenge the assertions they hear in their peers' presentations.

Big answer plenary	Ask students to reconsider the Big Question: *Where will people go on holiday in the future?* Ask students to come up with an answer to this question and at least one advantage or disadvantage of the destination they choose.

TRAVEL 6: What can go wrong on holiday?

Assessment objectives
AO6 Use vocabulary and sentence structures for clarity, purpose and effect, with accurate spelling and punctuation.

Non-exam assessment
- Silver Step component 1
- Gold Step component 1

Differentiated learning outcomes
- **Entry Level 1 students** should show some awareness of full stops and capital letters when writing about lost luggage.
- **Entry Level 2 students** should demarcate most sentences with full stops and capital letters when writing about lost luggage.
- **Entry Level 3 students** should use capital letters, full stops and question marks accurately when writing about lost luggage.
- **GCSE-ready students** should begin to develop punctuation within sentences when writing about lost luggage.

Resources
- **Worksheets**: 6.1, 6.2, 6.3, 6.4
- **PPT 6**: What can go wrong on holiday?

Big question
What can go wrong on holiday? Show students a video clip of travel disruption, for example: www.youtube.com/watch?v=4IrNIc5AJA0 . Ask students if they have ever experienced any problems when going on holiday or know of anyone who has.

Getting you thinking

Before the start of the lesson, cut up the slips on **Worksheet 6.1** and distribute one slip to each student in the class, so that each has a word appropriate to their level. Students move to one side of the room if they feel they would pack their item for a holiday, the other side of the room if they don't. Ask students to justify their choices.

Tell the students that they can only take a small number of items (e.g. three) in their luggage. The whole group should now work together to decide which items they take and which they leave behind.

Give extra support by…
…asking students to state whether the item they have would be useful or not.

Give extra challenge by…
… asking students to add in details about the holiday (such as expected weather conditions, ease of buying more supplies) and exploring how this affects their decision making.

Explore the skills

Display Slide 1 of **PPT 6**. Explain that a reasonably common problem people face on holiday is losing their luggage. Through Q&A, explore what issues this would cause for tourists.

Ask students to use **Worksheet 6.2** to explain what problems would be caused by losing each of the useful luggage items shown. Students must focus on including accurate punctuation.

Give extra support by…
… reminding students that each simple sentence must start with a capital letter and end with a full stop.

Give extra challenge by...

... encouraging students working at a higher level to use punctuation within sentences, such as apostrophes and commas.

Develop the skills

Distribute **Worksheet 6.3**, which gives advice on what to do if your luggage goes missing. Read through the advice several times. After each reading, check for comprehension and ask students what advice the leaflet gives for travellers who have lost their luggage. Make brief notes of their responses on the board.

Display Slide 2 of **PPT 6**. Tell students that they are now going to use the notes you have made on the board to create their own advice leaflet. On the board, model converting the advice students have found either into phrases (EL1) or full sentences (EL2, EL3 & GCSE-ready). Ask students to suggest possible punctuation for each phrase (EL1) or appropriate punctuation for each sentence (EL2, EL3 & GCSE-ready).

Give extra support by...
... assisting students to highlight key words in the text of **Worksheet 6.3** that indicate what someone who has lost their luggage should do.

Give extra challenge by...
... asking students to highlight the text of **Worksheet 6.3** as you read and only reading it through once.

Apply the skills

Ask students to look again at **Worksheet 6.3** and guide them through the format, highlighting features of a leaflet, such as illustrations, bullet points and subheadings.

Display Slide 3 of **PPT 6**. Now ask students to use the writing frame on **Worksheet 6.4** to prepare a poster advising people what to do if they lose their credit card or money. They can use Worksheet 6.3 as a model for the poster, and word banks are provided for Silver level students to help them with the new context. Encourage them to think of ways of making their poster eye-catching and easy to understand, while also punctuating their sentences correctly. When they have finalised their text, students can be encouraged to create a version using ICT. This will allow them to include design features such as different fonts and text sizes for headings, colour and images.

When they have finished, ask students to swap work with a partner and check that they have used punctuation correctly in their posters.

Give extra support by...
...giving hints about what you should do in this situation, e.g. call the police, call the bank or company that issued the credit card.

...using a trusted adult to check the students' work and supporting them in correcting any errors.

Give extra challenge by...
... encouraging students to adapt their writing to the form of a poster by using direct address and a clear layout.

Big answer plenary	Ask students to reconsider the Big Question: *What can go wrong on holiday?* Ask students how well they feel they would cope if they lost their luggage, money or passport on a holiday. Explore how well they feel they would cope with other problems that might occur while they are travelling.

VOLUNTEERING 1

Lending a hand

Assessment objectives

AO1 Read and understand a range of texts; identify and interpret explicit and implicit information and ideas.

AO2 Explain and comment on how writers use language and structure to achieve effects and influence readers, using relevant subject terminology to support views.

Non-exam assessment

- Silver Step component 1
- Gold Step component 1

Differentiated learning outcomes

- **Entry Level 1 students** should read some high-frequency and familiar words in a simple text about volunteering.
- **Entry Level 2 students** should read with some fluency and accuracy a text about volunteering.
- **Entry Level 3 students** should read a text about volunteering with fluency, accuracy and expression.
- **GCSE-ready students** should read and understand a range of texts about volunteering showing consideration to an audience.

Resources

- **Worksheets**: 1.1, 1.2
- **PPT 1**: Lending a hand

Big question — *What is volunteering?* Ask students what the word 'volunteer' means. Encourage them to give examples, such as running an errand for a neighbour or to helping out at a school event. Elicit through discussion that volunteering means offering to do something to help others that you will not be paid for. It means giving your time, skills and enthusiasm to something you think is worthwhile.

Getting you thinking

Reinforce with students that volunteering is about giving your time to a good cause. You don't get paid, but you do get the chance to use your talents, develop new skills, and experience the pleasure that comes from making a real difference to other people's lives, as well as your own. Make sure that students are aware that volunteering may be for a large charity or organisation, but it may equally be something as small as offering to carry books for you!

Ask students if any of them go to sports clubs or other out-of-school activities and discuss whether they think the people who run the activity are paid or are volunteers (many are likely to be run by volunteers).

Tell students they are going to watch a clip about volunteering, which can be accessed via Slide 1 of **PPT 1**. After the clip, ask students to suggest what type of things the students may have volunteered for. Lead the discussion about what could be fun, how they could help other people and what different forms volunteering can take – for example, offering time or skills, at home or abroad, and so on.

Give students a few examples, such as washing cars, packing food bags at Christmas, having a cake sale and running a marathon, and ask them for any other examples they can think of.

> **Give extra support by…**
> …asking students whether they have heard of Children in Need and Comic Relief. What sorts of things have people done as volunteers for those events in order to raise money or help good causes?

Explore the skills

Display Slide 2 from **PPT 1**. Read through the text with the students and ask questions to check that they have all understood it. Do they think the people who run the Friends of River Park are all volunteers? If so, why do they think that?

Distribute **Worksheet 1.1** and explain to students that they are going to read a poster prepared by the Friends of River Park with the aim of attracting more people to help with organising and running their fund-raising and other events. Guide students if necessary as they tackle the task by asking questions to lead them to the part of the text where they will find the answers.

Discuss students' answers with the group and, if appropriate, talk about the skill of scanning to find specific information within a text. You can reinforce this by providing a bus or train timetable for students to look at and highlight specific information that you request. For example, ask students go to the National Rail website (http://ojp.nationalrail.co.uk/service/timesandfares/BHM/WIN/tomorrow/1200/dep) to find out the quickest train from Birmingham to Winchester.

> **Give extra support by…**
> …reading the poster text with students.
>
> **Give extra challenge by…**
> …asking for other sorts of texts they might scan for information, e.g. cinema times.

Develop the skills

Ask students to look back at the poster on **Worksheet 1.1** and to think about how River Park try to persuade you to volunteer for them. Ask students, working in small groups, to tell you what it is about the poster that might make them want to volunteer. Ask them what the key words are that might appeal to the reader, e.g. 'kind', 'give some time', 'help', 'lend a hand', 'make new friends', 'see shows free', 'choose when you volunteer'.

> **Give extra support by…**
> …giving copies of the slide to those who request it so that they can highlight difficult words for clarification.

Apply the skills

Distribute **Worksheet 1.2** and allow students 10 minutes to work through the tasks.

> **Give extra support by…**
> …putting students into pairs to work on the tasks.
>
> **Give extra challenge by…**
> …asking students to note down two things they have learned so far about what makes a good volunteer.

Big answer plenary	*What is volunteering?* Students should now be able to come up with a fuller response to the question. Ask students whether they might now look for volunteering opportunities and what they would do.

VOLUNTEERING 2

Wanted – volunteers of all ages

Assessment objectives

AO5 Communicate clearly, effectively and imaginatively, selecting and adapting tone, style and register for different forms, purposes and audiences.

AO6 Use vocabulary and sentence structures for clarity, purpose and effect, with accurate spelling and punctuation.

Non-exam assessment
- Silver Step component 1
- Gold Step component 1

Differentiated learning outcomes
- **Entry Level 1 students** should show some awareness of full stops and capital letters in an email application for volunteering.
- **Entry Level 2 students** should demarcate most sentences with full stops and capital letters an email application for volunteering.
- **Entry Level 3 students** should use capital letters, full stops and question marks accurately in an email application for volunteering.
- **GCSE-ready students** should use full stops, capital letters, commas, speech marks and question marks accurately in an email application for volunteering.

Resources
- **Worksheets**: 2.1, 2.2
- **PPT 2**: Wanted – volunteers of all ages

Big question	*How can you volunteer?* Ask students if they have ever volunteered for anything. If they have, how did they get the 'job'? Did they see an advert in a paper, magazine or website? Did they go online to find a particular charity? Did a friend or relative ask them to help? Explain that there are many ways to volunteer.

Getting you thinking

Display Slide 1 from **PPT 2**. Remind students that volunteering is about giving your time to a good cause, without pay. Explain that there are thousands of volunteering opportunities. Then play the clip. After the clip, ask students what skills, personal qualities and experience they could bring to a volunteering role. Also ask what they can personally gain from volunteering. Explain to students that the clip they saw is only one of many organisations where they can find volunteering jobs.

> **Give extra support by…**
> …suggesting skills or experience students may already have, such as babysitting or looking after animals.

Explore the skills

Tell students they are going to look at an advertisement for volunteers for a dog show. The advert asks them to send an email if they want to volunteer. In pairs, give students 5 minutes to think about what other formats (ways) they might be asked to apply to be a volunteer. Each pair can then feed back to the group. Make sure they have included letter, application form, CV, telephone call and online form.

Explain that all written applications have certain features that need to be included. Ask what features are standard for an email, e.g. To, From and Subject. In the body of the email there should also be a greeting ('Dear [name]', 'Dear Sir/Madam') and close or way of signing off (e.g. 'Yours sincerely', 'Best wishes', 'Kind regards', depending on how formal the email is and how well you know the person you are writing to).

Explain that in any written communication it is very important that the meaning is clear, that all words are spelt correctly, and that grammar and punctuation are correct. Give students **Worksheet 2.1** and ask them to do Tasks 1 and 2.

> **Give extra support** by…
> …explaining that 'format' means the way something is arranged or laid out.
> …to Silver level students by reading the word 'charity' with them (**Worksheet 2.1**).
>
> **Give extra challenge** by…
> …giving students different spellings for wear/where, which/witch, here/hear, two/too and asking them to write a short sentence including each word.

Develop the skills

Ask students how they can check their spelling. Remind them of the use of dictionaries. For EL1/EL2 students, explain how to use first and second letters of words. Advise caution with spell checkers; point out that there are words in English that sound the same, but are spelt differently, e.g. see/sea, right/write/rite, their/there. Spell checkers may not pick up a misspelt word that exists in the language, e.g. 'I can sea you.' – 'Their is no milk left.' – 'I am going to right a letter.'

Remind students of the importance of punctuation: a capital letter at the start of a sentence; a capital letter for proper nouns, e.g. Birmingham; a full stop or question mark at the end of a sentence. Give an example: I am going home. Am I going home?

Give students **Worksheet 2.2**, which helps them plan their email. Suggest that they use **Worksheet 2.1** for details and check that all students understand what the tasks require them to do. Explain that they are not writing the actual email - this exercise is called 'drafting', i.e. preparing what they want to say before writing the final text. Give students 5 minutes to complete their draft.

> **Give extra support** by…
> …asking students if there are any other words they could use in their email and helping them to spell them.

Apply the skills

Now ask students to write the final draft of their email volunteering to help with 'Bark in the Park'. Hand out **Worksheet 2.3** and give students 10 minutes to prepare their final email.

> **Give extra support** by…
> …getting students to swap their emails to look for any spelling, punctuation and grammar errors.

Display Slide 2 from **PPT 2**. Tell students to use the links given there to find a national or local volunteering opportunity. If they don't have internet access, suggest other options such as a community centre or library noticeboard or Citizens Advice.

Once students have found a suitable opportunity, ask them to list the skills they think they would need for that role. Then ask them to think again about their own skills and experiences (as discussed in 'Getting you thinking') and which of these they could bring to this volunteering role.

Finally, ask students to write a list of the things they would put in an email to the organisation, e.g. saying who they are, why they want to apply, what skills and experience they have. (Write the points to be addressed on the board.) If time allows, you could hand out an adapted version of **Worksheet 2.3** for students to draft their email applying for this volunteering role.

Big answer plenary	*How can you volunteer?* Students should now be able to come up with an informed response to the question in respect of where to look for volunteering opportunities and the formats they can use to apply for volunteering 'jobs'.

VOLUNTEERING 3

People, animals and events

Assessment objectives

AO1 Read and understand a range of texts; identify and interpret explicit and implicit information and ideas.

Non-exam assessment
- Silver Step component 1
- Gold Step component 1

Differentiated learning outcomes

- **Entry Level 1 students** should use blending to decode some familiar and unfamiliar words in texts about volunteering.
- **Entry Level 2 students** should use appropriate strategies to decode unfamiliar words in texts about volunteering.
- **Entry Level 3 students** should use a range of strategies to tackle words in a variety of texts about volunteering.
- **GCSE-ready students** should use a range of strategies to tackle more difficult words in a variety of texts about volunteering.

Resources
- **Worksheets**: 3.1, 3.2
- **PPT 3**: Volunteering opportunities

Big question | *What types of opportunities are there for volunteering?* Ask students what type of opportunities they can think of for volunteering, such as helping people or animals, helping at an event, building or mending things or raising money for good causes.

Getting you thinking

Display Slide 1 from **PPT 3**. Explain to students they are going to see and listen to five people who are involved in different types of volunteering. Play the clip, then ask students which of the volunteering opportunities they would choose.

Tell students they can start volunteering at any age. For example, it might be helping at home with chores, walking a dog or babysitting. Explain that some organisations/charities will take volunteers from the age of 14, but that others need people to be 18 or older, especially if it is an opportunity to work abroad.

To demonstrate how much impact volunteering has on the world, go to www.projects-abroad.co.uk to see the countries that have volunteering projects and to get an idea of the type of projects.

> **Give extra support** by...
> ...playing the clip a second time and discussing what each person is doing.

Explore the skills

Tell students they are going to read about Jess and Holly, who want to become volunteers. Explain that there are techniques to help with reading, especially for unfamiliar words. All words start off as a root word – a basic word, e.g. 'happy' – and this word cannot be broken down into another word. If you put something in front of this word, you can change its meaning – e.g. 'unhappy'. Tell them that 'un-' is a prefix. Liken the word 'pre-' to something that happens at the start of or before an event, e.g. **pre**pare dinner or **pre**view a film. On the board write the prefixes 'up-', 'dis-' and 'in-'. Ask students in pairs to come up with two words for each prefix.

Tell students that as well as adding a prefix to a word, they can also put two words together to form a new word. Write on the board the words 'foot', 'him', 'under', 'air' and 'play'. Ask students in pairs to add a word to make a new word, e.g. 'football'.

Give students **Worksheet 3.1** to read and check understanding of all words.

> **Give extra challenge** by...
> ...reminding students to remember the technique of scanning, a way of reading that helps you to find specific information.
>
> ...explaining that you can change a word by adding letters or a word at the end of another word and that these are called suffixes. Put the suffixes '-ful', '-less', '-ly' on the board and ask students in pairs to come up with a word using these.

Develop the skills

Display Slide 2 from **PPT 3**. Give half the class some root words and the other half some prefixes and ask root word students to make a new word by pairing up with a prefix. Get students to move around the class, find a partner and then stand at the front of the class with them to show their new word and write their root word and prefix on the board.

Give each member of the class a root word – for example, 'foot', 'him', 'air', 'play', 'plane', 'ball', 'self', 'ground', 'port' and 'time' – and tell them to find another student with a root word that makes up a new word.

Give students **Worksheet 3.2** to use in conjunction with **Worksheet 3.1**. Allow ten minutes for this task.

> **Give extra support** by...
> ...reminding students that a root word is a word that cannot be broken down into any other word.
>
> **Give extra challenge** by...
> ...asking students to identify more root words – words that cannot be broken down to make other words – and combine them into new words.

Apply the skills

Display Slide 3 from **PPT 3**. Explain to students that they are going to watch a clip and then play a game putting together prefixes and suffixes with root words. Tell them to watch carefully as it will give them some clues.

Give students the three sets of cards shown on **Worksheet 3.3**.

- prefix cards: re-, un-, sub-, dis-, under-
- suffix cards: -ed, -er, -ness, -able, -ful, -ing, -less
- root words: kind, like, do, way, agree, ground, care, play

Put students in mixed-ability groups and tell them to make up as many words as they can using the sets of cards. Suggest that students write down the words as some of the prefixes and suffixes can be used more than once. Ask each group to feed their words back to the class. This can be made into a competition between the groups.

> **Give extra support** by...
> ...demonstrating how to make up a word using the cards.
>
> **Give extra challenge** by...
> ...thinking of other root words to which they can add the prefixes and suffixes.

Big answer plenary	*What types of opportunities are there for volunteering?* Students should now be able to come up with a more informed response to the question. Have they come across any opportunities that might appeal to them, either now or in the future?

VOLUNTEERING 4

Recruiting volunteers

Assessment objectives

AO5 Communicate clearly, effectively and imaginatively, selecting and adapting tone, style and register for different forms, purposes and audiences.

Non-exam assessment
- Silver Step component 1
- Gold Step component 1

Differentiated learning outcomes
- **Entry Level 1 students** should try to match writing to structure within a scaffolded form when advertising for volunteers.
- **Entry Level 2 students** should show some awareness of non-narrative form and audience within a given structure when advertising for volunteers.
- **Entry Level 3 students** should sometimes adapt writing style to match purpose and audience, and sequence ideas logically when advertising for volunteers.
- **GCSE-ready students** should organise writing appropriately for the purpose of the reader and sequence ideas often in a sustained, developed and interesting way when advertising for volunteers.

Resources
- **Worksheets**: 4.1, 4.2
- **PPT 4**: Recruiting volunteers

Big question | *How can I find volunteers?* Suggest to students that finding volunteers is no different from looking for people to fill job vacancies. Ask students what they think employers do to find staff, e.g. advertise jobs in newspapers, magazines and on radio, and via online recruitment companies. Then ask students what other ways there are to find people, e.g. word of mouth, friends, family, YouTube, social media.

Getting you thinking

Display Slide 1 from **PPT 4**. Play the clip. Promote discussion by asking students if the clip made them feel that they could volunteer by just doing simple tasks such as playing bingo with someone – or even just keeping an older person company. Suggest to them that people may think volunteering is a huge commitment when in fact simple things can mean a lot. Ask students whether this clip would persuade someone to volunteer. If, for example, this appeared on social media, do they feel it would make people think and possibly volunteer?

> **Give extra support** by…
> …playing the clip a second time to remind students of the different things that volunteers could do.

Explore the skills

Explain to students that, when people are looking for volunteers, they not only need to use the right medium (e.g. a newspaper advertisement, a poster or leaflet, or a post on Twitter), but also need to make sure that the message is communicated in an appropriate way. The language used must appeal to the people they are trying to attract. Give the example that a formal letter posted on Facebook may not appeal to younger users, while a letter in text speak sent through the post may turn many people off. Explain how important it is to get the right writing style for the form and the audience.

> **Give extra support** by…
> …explaining that the audience refers to those people that the writers of the advert, poster, leaflet, etc. are trying to attract – in this case, volunteers.

Give extra challenge by...
...asking students to think about the difference between formal and informal language and give an example of when each would be used.

Develop the skills

Display Slide 2 from **PPT 4**. Explain to students that when trying to attract people, they must make sure that their writing style is appropriate and the spelling, punctuation and grammar are correct. They will also need to write in sentences. Go through the examples on the slide. Ask students to write an example of each type of phrase or sentence, at the level appropriate to them: simple sentence for EL1 and EL2, compound sentence for EL3 and complex sentence for GCSE-ready students.

Explain that for many types of advert, paragraphs are important. Explain how a simple advert could just have three paragraphs: a beginning, middle and end.

Ask students to complete the tasks on **Worksheet 4.1a** and **b**, using words and phrases (EL1), simple sentences (EL2), compound sentences (EL3) or complex sentences (GCSE-ready). Then distribute **Worksheet 4.2** and allow students about 15 minutes to complete it.

Give extra support by...
...telling Silver level students that there are some blank spaces on the word grid to add extra words that you can spell for them.

Give extra challenge by...
...asking students to swap application forms to spot any mistakes, comment on the sentence structure and check it is in a logical order.

Apply the skills

Display Slide 3 from **PPT 4**. Explain that there are various conjunctions and refer to the slide. Put students into Silver and Gold ability groups. Explain that they are going to make up sentences using conjunctions. Silver students will work with the coordinating conjunctions in the top row of the PPT Slide 3 table to create compound sentences; Gold students will work with these and the subordinating conjunctions to create compound and complex sentences. First, a member of the group says a sentence and the next person in the group has to add a conjunction and another sentence and then the next member another conjunction and sentence until everyone has added a conjunction and a sentence.

Print out the slide and cut up the connectives. Give Silver level students 'and', 'so', 'or', 'but', and Gold level students the remainder. Still working in their groups, the students should now write three sentences saying why it is good to volunteer for something. You could suggest specific types of volunteering to help prompt students, e.g. helping to run a lunch club for year 7, helping to clean up a local park or helping an elderly person do their shopping. When students have finished, ask them to swap their writing with other groups to identify the conjunctions and sentence structure.

Give extra support by...
...giving more examples of the use of simple conjunctions.

Give extra challenge by...
...asking students to write a sentence with each of the types of conjunctions.

Big answer plenary	*How can I find volunteers?* Ask students what they know now about finding volunteers in respect of the writing style and content of an advertisement. Ask them what is important about the content and structure of any communication if they are going to look like a professional organisation.

VOLUNTEERING 5

The benefits of volunteering

Assessment objectives

AO1 Read and understand a range of texts: identify and interpret explicit and implicit information and ideas.

AO4 Evaluate texts and support this with appropriate textual references.

Non-exam assessment
- Silver Step component 1
- Gold Step component 1

Differentiated learning outcomes

- **Entry Level 1 students** should locate some points and information in simple texts about the benefits of volunteering.
- **Entry Level 2 students** should locate main points and information in texts about the benefits of volunteering.
- **Entry Level 3 students** should locate key points in texts about the benefits of volunteering.
- **GCSE-ready students** should locate and use ideas and information about the benefits of volunteering.

Resources
- **Worksheets**: 5.1, 5.2
- **PPT 5**: Benefits of volunteering

Big question — *What are the benefits of volunteering?* Ask students what they think the benefits are. Suggest that they think about things such as learning new skills, meeting new people and gaining experience of fundraising or helping people.

Getting you thinking

Display Slide 1 from **PPT 5**. Tell students they are going to watch a clip about people talking about the benefits of volunteering in sport. Play the clip. Then encourage discussion and ask students what were the benefits that people in the clip mentioned, e.g. new skills that might help to get promotion, using your talents, giving something back to the community. Ask them if there is any sport or other activity that they think they could volunteer for. How might it help them in the future for getting a job or promotion? Allow up to ten minutes for the discussion.

Give extra support by…
…playing the clip a second time to remind students of the different things that the volunteers said.

Explore the skills

Suggest to students that when they are reading some texts and there are words that they do not usually come across every day, there are ways to work out such unfamiliar words in texts. Tell them that a dictionary is always a good place to start, but if they don't have one or cannot get access online, there are other ways. Tell them that these are called context clues. Ask more confident students if they know or can guess what a context clue is.

Give extra support by…
…explaining that context means the setting, the background.

Give extra challenge by…
…asking students to find out what synonyms and antonyms are.

Develop the skills

Display Slide 2 from **PPT 5**. Ask students to look at the slide and spend a couple of minutes, individually or in pairs, thinking what the answer to the riddle is and, more importantly, how they got to the answer. Ask for a show of hands who guessed it was 'sun'. Ask students how they arrived at this answer. Explain that this context clue is known as inference. The conclusion is based on evidence in the context that it was a lovely day, they were playing outside and it was warm? So what is the mystery object? The sun.

Explain that another clue is an antonym or a contrasting/opposite word, e.g. 'Unlike Jen, who was easy-going, Jackie was very nervy.' Ask what 'nervy' might mean, the opposite of easy-going.

Explain that another clue is a synonym where two similar words are used in a sentence, e.g. 'Santa Claus was so portly that his doctor told him he was overweight.'

Give students **Worksheet 5.1**. Tell them to complete the task(s) on this worksheet. If they are unsure of any words, encourage them to think about the clues in the text. Ask students to highlight the words for which they had to use contextual clues in order to work out the meaning. Give students 15 minutes to complete the worksheet.

Now give them **Worksheet 5.2** to complete. Remind students that, as well as using context clues, they can break down words with prefixes and/or suffixes to uncover the possible meaning. Allow 10 minutes for the worksheet tasks.

> **Give extra support** by…
> …writing the examples on the board and underlining the relevant words.

Apply the skills

Display Slide 3 from **PPT 5**. Put students into groups. Explain that each group has three words and that they must find a synonym (similar word) and antonym (opposite word) for each word – it must be a new word and not one found by changing the word using a prefix or suffix (e.g. active/inactive). Silver level students should work on Group A words, while Gold level students should work on words from Goups B and C. Put a name for each group on the board with their words. Tell students to put their hands up when their group has found the words. Ask them for their answers and write these on the board.

When each group has done this, tell them they must now write a simple sentence using both the original word and the synonym; they should then do the same using the original word and the antonym. Ask Gold level students to act as scribes. Ask students to read out their sentences to the other groups.

> **Give extra support** by…
> …suggesting students look up the meaning of the words in the dictionary.
> …giving the example of 'un-' for 'unhappy' and '-ed' for 'walked' as prefixes and suffixes so that Silver level students have an understanding of the instruction.
>
> **Give extra challenge** by…
> …giving students a piece of text from their course to find contextual clues.

Big answer plenary	*What are the benefits of volunteering?* Now that they have completed the tasks, ask students what the benefit would be to them personally of volunteering and what type of volunteering would help them to gain these benefits, such as organising an event, working with people or helping out in the community.

VOLUNTEERING 6

Valuable volunteers

Assessment objectives

AO7 Demonstrate presentation skills.

AO8 **Listen and respond appropriately to spoken language, including to questions and feedback on presentations.**

AO9 Use spoken English effectively in speeches and presentations.

Non-exam assessment
- Silver Step component 1
- Gold Step component 1

Differentiated learning outcomes

- **Entry Level 1 students** should be able to engage with others when discussing volunteering.
- **Entry Level 2 students** should be able to engage with others, making simple comments and suggestions when discussing volunteering.
- **Entry Level 3 students** should respond to others, developing ideas and making helpful comments and suggestions when discussing volunteering.
- **GCSE-ready students** should make contributions and ask questions that are responsive to others' views and ideas when discussing volunteering.

Resources
- **Worksheets**: 6.1, 6.2
- **PPT 6**: Valuable volunteers

Big question — *What makes a good volunteer?* Ask students the question. Get them thinking about personal qualities, such as being happy, fun, awesome, responsible, reliable and caring. Then ask what other things need to be considered, e.g. interpersonal skills, communication skills, being non-judgemental and adaptable to diverse cultures.

Getting you thinking

Display Slide 1 from **PPT 6**. Tell students that these are some of the skills or personality traits that volunteers need, depending on the voluntary work they are doing. Ask students why they think listening is a skill that volunteers need (e.g. to listen to and take instructions, being with people who just need to chat).

Explain that, in addition to these, presentation skills comprise another key skill needed by many volunteers. At the end of a project, volunteers may have to make a presentation to a charity or trust, e.g. about the progress that has been made, what funds have been used, what is happening at the moment and what they hope to do in the future. This could be for a large project, e.g. building water wells in underdeveloped countries or developing a skate park for the local community, or something on a smaller scale, such as reporting back about volunteering activities in, say, a school charity day.

> **Give extra support** by…
> …explaining that presentation skills are about talking to someone or a group of people clearly and effectively in order to get your message across.

Explore the skills

Discuss with students what they think is involved in making a speech or a presentation. Ask them to make a list of all the things they need to consider. Ask more confident students to read out their lists. Make sure they have covered: preparing material on a PowerPoint or handouts; using correct punctuation, spelling and grammar in their material; making the presentation interesting, entertaining (depending on the subject and audience) and informative. Remind students of the need to practise a presentation to get the tone, pace, volume and intonation correct. Give students an example of someone saying something first in a really boring tone, and then too quickly or slowly. Give them an example of someone who is too softly spoken and hesitant, as opposed to a well-paced and confident tone.

> **Give extra support** by…
> …giving more examples of tone, pace, volume and intonation.
>
> **Give extra challenge** by…
> …asking them to write a two-minute speech to give at a parents' evening at school about an activity that went well during the year, e.g. a sports or fund-raising event.

Develop the skills

Display Slide 2 from **PPT 6**. Tell students that the YouTube clip outlines things you should and shouldn't do when making a presentation. Remind students that not only does the material and the way it is presented have to be suitable for the audience, but their body language (non-verbal communication) should be appropriate too.

Give students **Worksheet 6.1** to complete in 15 minutes. Go through each example of body language and see if students have the same interpretation. Explain to students that after a speech or presentation, they are likely to be asked questions. Tell them that the way they respond to questions, verbally and non-verbally, is as important as the presentation itself. Explain that they should listen to others, take turns in responding and be prepared to make contributions. It is OK to agree or disagree with a comment, but if they disagree, they should have an alternative suggestion to offer.

> **Give extra support** by…
> …giving a demonstration of each type of body language on **Worksheet 6.1**.
>
> **Give extra challenge** by…
> …asking students to show how they would demonstrate each non-verbal feature to a child, to show the meaning of the matching word.

Apply the skills

Display Slide 3 from **PPT 6**. Tell students they are going to plan and prepare a presentation about becoming a volunteer. Go through the five slides and discuss the sort of information that could be included for each one. **Worksheet 6.2** gives them further help and a framework to use. Put Silver level students in pairs and explain that, while they need to do individual presentations, they can work together to discuss ideas, words to use and how to present their ideas. Suggest Silver level students use words and pictures if they have access to the internet. This activity will take at least 20 minutes and can be done in more than one lesson.

Ask more confident students to give their presentations for questions and feedback.

> **Give extra support** by…
> …discussing with students the questions on the slide before they start their planning so that they have an understanding of what each slide requires.
>
> **Give extra challenge** by…
> …asking students who gave a presentation how they would change it or their style of presentation as a result of any questions and feedback. If they used PowerPoint, ask whether they found that helpful or whether they would prefer just to use notes.

Big answer plenary	*What makes a good volunteer?* Ask students why being able to make effective speeches and presentations can be an essential quality in some volunteering roles. Talk about funding, continuing a project, repeating a project and so on.

ADVENTURE 1

Race to the Pole

Assessment objectives

AO1 Read and understand a range of texts: identify and interpret explicit and implicit information and ideas.

Non-exam assessment
- Silver Step component 2
- Gold Step component 2

Differentiated learning outcomes
- **Entry Level 1 students** should locate some points and information in simple adventure texts.
- **Entry Level 2 students** should locate the main points and information in adventure texts.
- **Entry Level 3 students** should locate key points in adventure texts.
- **GCSE-ready students** should locate and use ideas and information and refer to the adventure text to support their ideas.

Resources
- **Worksheets**: 1.1, 1.2
- **PPT 1**: Race to the Pole

Big question | *Who won the race to the South Pole?* Explain that an adventure is an unusual, exciting or daring experience. Adventurers are often explorers who love the challenge of trying to go somewhere where very few people – if any – have been before. Ask students if they are aware that in 1911 there was a race between two explorers to reach the South Pole. If any students have heard of it, ask them to outline what happened to the rest of the class. If students are not aware of it, explain that two men wanted to be the first person to reach the South Pole, a place where no human had been before.

Getting you thinking

Display Slide 1 from **PPT 1**. Tell students they are going to watch the introduction of a video clip about the race. Play the clip (up to 1.42 minutes). Ask students who they think might win the race, Scott or Amundsen, and ask them to give reasons why.

> **Give extra support** by…
> … explaining that an expedition is an organised trip by a group of people.
>
> **Give extra challenge** by…
> …asking questions about the two men's characters.

Explore the skills

Ask students what they thought were the main points they can recall from the clip – for example, two men, two teams, one goal (to reach the South Pole) – and why they remembered these points. Write their answers on the board. Discuss with students why they think these were the main points made in the video.

Explain to students that when they watch a video clip, not only are they listening to what is being said, but they also have visual images to support what they are hearing. When they read a text, the challenge is a little different. Explain that when they read a text, the students should pretend to be detectives. Their challenge is to find the main point as well as other key points, and to look for clues about what the text is about. For example, they should consider what main point is made at the start of the text – does it tell you what the text is about? What other points (key points) in the text tell you more about the main point?

Give extra support by…
…playing the clip a second time.

Give extra challenge by…
…asking students to summarise what the clip was about.

Develop the skills

Explain that in a text, the main point can normally be found at the beginning. Refer back to the main points on the board and explore with students what might make a good opening for a brief text about the race to the South Pole. With Gold level students explain how a new paragraph is created when there is a change of **t**ime, **p**erson, **t**opic or **p**lace (summarised in the acronym TiPToP). It will help students to find key points if they look at the first sentence of each paragraph.

Display Slide 2 from **PPT 1**. Tell students that they are first going to read about another British explorer, Ernest Shackleton, who had tried to reach the South Pole before Scott and Amundsen. Read through the text with students or ask a confident student to read it aloud. Then look again at the text and show students how the text starts with key information: he was a British explorer (important background to who he was) who tried twice to get to the Pole (what he tried to do). The text then goes on to give more details.

Tell students they are going to read about the race to the Pole and find out more about the two men, Scott and Amundsen, who were in competition with each other. Explain that the two men had very different ways of getting ready for the expedition. Scott took the role as head of the team, ordered his people around and told them what they had to do. He decided what they were going to take with them, where they would set up camps and how they would travel across the snow. Amundsen talked to his team to discuss how they would do things. He also made sure that his team were well looked after and discussed things with them.

Give students **Worksheet 1.1**. Check their understanding of the text.

Give extra support by…
…recapping with students the different approaches taken by the two men.

Apply the skills

Display Slide 3 of **PPT 1**. Tell students to read **Worksheet 1.1** again and now think about what the two men might have been feeling on their journey, e.g. tired, cross, mad, happy, scared. Ask them again what they think happened at the end of the race, based on what they have read. For example: Who do they think won the race? Why did X lose? What could X have done to win?

Give students **Worksheet 1.2**. Allow 10 minutes for students to complete the tasks. Then go through answers. Were students able to pick out the main and key points?

Give extra support by…
…talking through the sequence of events with students.

Give extra challenge by…
…asking Gold level students to summarise **Worksheet 1.1** and to refer to the text to explain their views.

Big answer plenary	*Who won the race to the South Pole?* By a show of hands, see which of the two explorers students think won the race to the Pole. Ask students to give reasons why they thought it would be that person before telling or confirming the answer.

ADVENTURE 2

Why the Norwegians won the race

Assessment objectives
AO3 Compare writers' ideas and perspectives.

Non-exam assessment
- Silver Step component 2
- Gold Step component 2

Differentiated learning outcomes
- **Entry Level 1 students** should identify a similarity or difference between descriptions of an event in simple texts.
- **Entry Level 2 students** should identify a similarity or difference between character, events or presentation from simple texts.
- **Entry Level 3 students** should identify several similarities and differences between presentations of an event.
- **GCSE-ready students** should identify similarities and differences between significant events.

Resources
- **Worksheets**: 2.1, 2.2
- **PPT 2**: Great Britain vs Norway

Big question | *Why did the Norwegians win the race?* Tell students that to answer this question, they need to look at the way the two explorers approached the planning of the trip and the way the different teams worked together. Show how easy it can be to pick out similarities and difference when you look at something. Ask students with dark hair to go to the right of the class and students with fair hair to go to the left. Ask what is similar and what is different about the students – for example, all the students in one group have brown hair, but some of these will have blue eyes and some have brown eyes.

Getting you thinking

Display Slide 1 from **PPT 2**. Explain to students that they will see more of the clip about the race to the Pole that they watched in the previous lesson.

Tell students that during the clip they should listen out for the different approaches taken by Scott and Amundsen in preparing for the expedition. Give students a sheet of paper with two columns, headed 'Scott' and 'Amundsen', and ask them to note down words (Gold level students) or draw quick sketches (Silver level students) to remind them of anything they spot about the preparation and running of the expedition.

Now run the clip from where you stopped in Lesson 1 (1:42) to the end. Pause the clip at key moments to give students time to write down words or draw quick sketches. Depending on students' level of ability, it might be an idea to put them in pairs, with one focusing on Scott and one on Amundsen.

Give extra support by...

...adding key headings onto the sheet of paper with the two columns to help guide students' responses, e.g. *From..., Aim, Use of dogs, Food, Team*.

Give extra challenge by...

...asking students to make initial notes of any similarities and differences between the two explorers' preparation for the expedition.

Explore the skills

Explain to students that they are going to be making comparisons between Scott's and Amundsen's expeditions. They can practise first by undertaking an easy comparison task. Display Slide 2 of **PPT 2**. In pairs ask students to list the similarities and differences between the flags: for example, both have the colours red, white and blue; both fly on a flag pole; both are the same overall shape (rectangle); however, they have different patterns; one has more blue than the other; one has more lines, etc. Through discussion, ensure all students understand the distinction between similarities and differences.

> **Give extra support** by…
> …writing on the board, in columns, the similarities and differences of the flags to reinforce the points.
>
> **Give extra challenge** by…
> …telling students to go to the following website, which has a useful compilation of flags, and select two flags to compare: www.sciencekids.co.nz/pictures/flags.html

Develop the skills

Explain to students that when they look for similarities and differences in a text, they are looking for things that are either the same or are different. This could be to do with people, places, events, products, ideas, and so on. Tell students that the key to making successful comparisons between texts is to have an organised way of finding and identifying clues.

Display Slide 3 from **PPT 2** and make sure students are clear about how a Venn diagram works. Replicate the slide on the board. Going back to the notes students made from the clip, ask for similarities (e.g. both are men, they are explorers, they want to reach the South Pole, they each want to be the first to get there). Write these in the central shape where the circles overlap. Now ask for differences and write them in the outer shapes. For example, Scott was very formal, raced for 10+ hours a day, didn't test equipment, didn't prepare for bad weather, thought dogs weren't usable; Amundsen was less formal with his team, worked alongside them, used dog sledges to carry supplies, ensured there were supplies for the return journey, used the word 'we' rather than 'you', only raced for 5–6 hours a day.

Complete the Venn diagram on the board. Then give students **Worksheet 2.1**. Check their understanding of the text and clarify any difficult words.

> **Give extra support** by…
> …telling students to look for the same word used in each text on the worksheet, or for words that have a similar meaning.
>
> **Give extra challenge** by…
> …asking students for other ways they can identify similarities and differences in two texts, e.g. highlighting the words, drawing up lists of words with similar meanings.

Apply the skills

Distribute **Worksheet 2.2**, which will give students support in comparing the two texts on **Worksheet 2.1**. When they have finished, go through the students' answers and their explanations of what is similar and what is different. Confident students can present their findings to the class.

Big answer plenary	*Why did the Norwegians win the race?* Students should now be able to feed back that they were better prepared, they worked as a team, they used dog sledges, etc.

ADVENTURE 3

A passion for climbing

Assessment objectives
AO2 Explain and comment on how writers use language and structure to achieve effects and influence readers, using relevant subject terminology to support views.

AO6 Use vocabulary and sentence structures for clarity, purpose and effect, with accurate spelling and punctuation.

Non-exam assessment
- Silver Step component 2
- Gold Step component 2

Differentiated learning outcomes
- **Entry Level 1 students** should establish the meaning of a simple word in a narrative text.
- **Entry Level 2 students** should use contextual clues to help understand the meaning of simple words/language choices in a narrative text.
- **Entry Level 3 students** should identify some features of the language used by the writer of a narrative text.
- **GCSE-ready students** should begin to show awareness of the writer's craft in a narrative text.

Resources
- **Worksheets**: 3.1, 3.2
- **PPT 3**: A passion for climbing

Big question | *Would you risk losing your life?* The famous climber, Joe Simpson, has risked his life a thousand times because he is passionate about climbing. Ask students if there is any dangerous sport they really love already, or would love to do. Would they deliberately put themselves in danger to win or achieve something?

Getting you thinking

Display Slide 1 from **PPT 3**. Tell students they are going to watch a clip about Joe Simpson and some of the dangers he faced during his climbing career.

When the clip is finished, ask students what they felt when they were watching it. Do they think Joe Simpson is an action man, a hero? Why / Why not?

Tell students that he has now stopped climbing and turned to writing books about the extreme dangers he has faced. Ask if this still makes him a hero. Explain that Joe always tries hard to help his readers picture the scene and imagine what it was like to be in those situations.

> **Give extra support by…**
> …asking students to think of describing words that Joe might use in a book about climbing mountains.

Explore the skills

Explain to students that, as a new writer, Joe has had to think a lot about how he can help the reader get a clear picture of what he is writing about.

Display Slide 2 of **PPT 3** and explain that Joe Simpson has decided to write a story about his climbing exploits, to be read out to primary school children. Through a short discussion (up to 5 minutes), elicit some of the features of writing that would be important in a story for this age group – for example:

- It must grab their attention.
- It must be clear and easy enough to understand.
- The words must help to create an image in the children's minds.

Which of the sentences on the slide do they think Joe would choose to write? Read through the sentences one by one and as a whole class discuss whether each would be a good choice. Encourage students to try and explain why they think that – for example:

- It makes climbing sound exciting.
- It's a bit dull.
- It describes the snow very well.

Ask students to work in pairs for five minutes to pick out all the describing words. Silver level students can focus on just the shorter sentences at the top of the slide.

Then spend five minutes discussing the text about the avalanche, and how the rest of the sentence can help you to understand what the word 'avalanche' means.

Give extra challenge by…
…asking students to come up with alternative adjectives.

Develop the skills

Give students **Worksheet 3.1** and ask students to read the text, which has been written from the viewpoint of Joe Simpson. Explain that Joe and his friend Simon Yates were on their way down from one of the highest peaks in the Andes mountains in South America. They were the first people ever to do this particular climb. The text describes what happened on the way down. Check understanding of the text as necessary and discuss ideas for a good title. Allow 10 minutes for this activity.

Give extra support by…
…showing students the video clip from the link on Slide 1 of PPT 3 for a second time and talking through some of the issues associated with climbing at that height, e.g. freezing temperatures, lack of oxygen.

Give extra challenge by…
…asking students to research other climbs by Joe Simpson.

Apply the skills

Give students **Worksheet 3.2**. Allow 10 minutes for students to complete the initial tasks, then check and compare answers.

Before they tackle the final task, display Slide 3 of **PPT 3** and ask students to describe to you what they see. Encourage them to tell you how it makes them feel, as well as describing the scene. Write words on the board that students can refer to as they tackle the final task.

Give extra support by…
…giving your own description and saying how it makes you feel.

Give extra challenge by…
…asking students to write a short story based on events that might have taken place in the mountains as shown on the slide.

Big answer plenary	*Would you risk losing your life?* Ask students whether they would prefer to be a climber or writer? Having seen a little of Joe's experience on the mountain, do they think it is worth risking your life for the thrill of climbing? Ask what type of person you need to be to take these risks and discuss how family and friends might feel about it.

ADVENTURE 4

In search of adventure

Assessment objectives
AO1 Read and understand a range of texts: identify and interpret explicit and implicit information and ideas.

Non-exam assessment
- Silver Step component 2
- Gold Step component 2

Differentiated learning outcomes
- **Entry Level 1 students** should locate some points and information in simple texts.
- **Entry Level 2 students** should locate the main points and information in texts.
- **Entry Level 3 students** should be able to locate key points in texts.
- **GCSE-ready students** should locate and use ideas and information in texts.

Resources
- **Worksheets**: 4.1
- **PPT 4**: In search of adventure
- Printed resources: travel brochures, telephone directories, travel guides, train timetables, cookery books or travel guides, food menus, newspaper articles

Big question — *How can you find adventure?* Ask students if they would like to go on an adventure like Captain Scott's trek to the South Pole, climber Joe Simpson up a mountain, or perhaps on a mission with adventurer and TV presenter Bear Grylls. Encourage all students to think of one adventure they would like to go on.

Getting you thinking

Display Slide 1 from **PPT 4**. Tell students they are going to watch people who set off on an adventure that involved walking, trekking, climbing and camping on a Scottish island. Ask students to think about what kind of adventure they would like to do while they are watching the clip. Play the clip (which could be cut off after three minutes) and then give students a couple of minutes to think about a possible adventure.

Explain to students that they are going to plan an adventure – it can be based on what they have just watched or can be entirely their own idea. Ask each student what adventure they would like to plan and write on the board the name and adventure of each student.

Put students in pairs and tell them to discuss and then agree on an adventure to plan together. Tell students to make some initial notes about their planned adventure. Allow a maximum of 5 minutes for this.

> **Give extra support** by…
> …asking what students are interested in, in order to help them decide on an adventure.
>
> **Give extra challenge** by…
> …asking students to describe to the class what adventure they are going to plan.

Explore the skills

Display Slide 2 from **PPT 4**. Explain to students that they need to find out quite a lot of information to plan their adventure. Often they will look on the internet, but sometimes the internet is not available and they will need to find information in other ways. Encourage a discussion about where they might look and write the suggestions on the board, e.g. libraries, magazines, travel agents, newspapers, TV guides.

> **Give extra support** by…
> …suggesting the type of information that can be found in a library, e.g. travel guides.
>
> **Give extra challenge** by…
> …asking students what type of information can be found in a library that is relevant to an adventure, e.g. maps.

Develop the skills

Ask students how they find the information they want when looking in a book or magazine. What tools can they use to find information more quickly? Give students some resources, e.g. travel brochures, telephone directories, travel guides, train timetables. Put students into small groups and ask them to think about what tools there are. Ask for feedback from each group and write suggestions on the board.

Display Slide 3 of **PPT 4**. Refer to the slide and the four main tools. Check against students' answers to see which of these tools they identified. Go through the slide and ask students for examples of each. Have a cookery/travel book, food menu and an article to show students to demonstrate the points.

Give students **Worksheet 4.1**.

> **Give extra support** by…
> …comparing a contents page and an index.
>
> **Give extra challenge** by…
> …asking student when headings are used as a tool, e.g. in an application form, in an information sheet, as the subject in an email.

Apply the skills

Tell students that now they know where to look to find the information, they need to plan their adventure. Tell students, working in their original pairs, to write down a list of the places they will go to for information for their particular adventure that is not internet based, e.g. in a library, in magazines, at a travel agent.

Now ask students what tools they will use for each book/magazine, e.g. use a contents page to find the chapter about a topic or place they want to find out about, use an index to find the page for a particular piece of information.

Ask students to make a list of all the things they need to consider when planning an adventure. Draw a spider diagram on the board with 'Adventure' in the centre and then ask students what they need to consider, e.g. money, where to go, what to do, how long for, means of travel, who with. This can be turned into a project to plan an actual adventure.

> **Give extra support** by…
> …selecting a topic in a book and helping students to find which chapter and page they need to go to.
>
> **Give extra challenge** by…
> …asking students to look in a specialist magazine and locate the key points that are applicable to the adventure they want to plan.

Big answer plenary	*How can you find an adventure?* Ask students the question again; they should be able to tell you where they can go for information and how to locate the specific information they need.

ADVENTURE 5

Survival

Assessment objectives

AO5 Communicate clearly, effectively and imaginatively, selecting and adapting tone, style and register for different forms, purposes and audiences

AO6 **Use vocabulary and sentence structures for clarity, purpose and effect, with accurate spelling and punctuation.**

Non-exam assessment
- Silver Step component 2
- Gold Step component 2

Differentiated learning outcomes
- **Entry Level 1 students** show some awareness of full stops and capital letters.
- **Entry Level 2 students** should demarcate most sentences with full stops and capital letters.
- **Entry Level 3 students** should use capital letters, full stops and question marks accurately.
- **GCSE-ready students** should use full stops, capital letters, commas, speech marks and question marks accurately.

Resources
- **Worksheets**: 5.1, 5.2, 5.3 (EL2 & EL3 only)
- **PPT 5**: Life of a castaway

Big question — *What do you need to survive?* Tell students to imagine they have been shipwrecked and washed up on a deserted island. Ask if any students have seen one of the reality TV programmes that feature such a scenario. If so, what can they remember about the problems faced? Have a discussion about the type of things they would need to do, e.g. find clean water, make a shelter, catch fish and so on.

Getting you thinking

Display Slide 1 from **PPT 5**. Ask students what thoughts and feelings the photo brings to mind. Some will probably think it looks a perfect holiday place – but ask students to think how it would be if they were there on their own, having been shipwrecked, and had to find a way to survive. Go round the class asking everyone to say three items that they would miss, e.g. phone, money, make-up, music, clothes, food, friends, family. How long and how well would they survive without these things?

Give extra support by…
…telling students the three things you would miss before they give their answers.

Explore the skills

Tell students to imagine that, after several days, they find an old glass bottle washed up on the beach. They are going to write a message to put in the bottle. Check that students understand the phrase 'message in a bottle'. Their letter is going to ask for help, for someone to come and rescue them.

Display Slide 2 from **PPT 5**. Remind students they are going to write a letter and they need to be able to describe their 'plight' in a logical order that is easy to understand (and in paragraphs for GCSE-ready students). Using the slide, explain about simple and compound sentences and using connecting words such as 'and' and 'but'.

Give extra support by…
…giving students simple sentences to join with 'and' or 'but'.

Give extra challenge by…
…asking students to think of other words that can connect two sentences.

Develop the skills

Distribute **Worksheet 5.1**, which helps students to plan the letter. Discuss with students the type of things they will put in their letter, e.g. what happened to them, where they think they are, what they are doing, what they can hear, what they can see, why they want to be rescued, etc. Write any words that are above the level on the board for students to refer to, e.g. deserted, shipwreck, island.

Ask students to draft out the letter to help them get their thoughts in order and to check any spellings before they do the final draft.

> **Give extra support** by…
> …helping students to structure the sentences on their draft.
>
> **Give extra challenge** by…
> …telling students before they write their letter to do a plan and then a draft. Suggest they do a spider diagram for the plan (as on Worksheet 5.1 EL3); the draft is then an extension of the plan with outline sentences.

Apply the skills

Distribute **Worksheet 5.2** and ask students to write the final version of their letter. Suggest to Gold level students that they use each point on their worksheet as a new paragraph.

Explain the importance of getting the message right, with correct spellings, so that whoever finds the bottle can understand the message. Ask students to swap letters with a partner and to check for correct use of capital letters, full stops and question marks, as well as correct spelling.

To take this learning further, explain to students that many spelling mistakes are made because words that sound the same are spelt differently depending on what is being said. Give the example of 'to'/'too'/'two'. Ask Gold level students to explain the difference. Ask EL2 and EL3 learners to complete the homophones spelling activities on their version of **Worksheet 5.3**. (This activity is not appropriate for Entry Level 1 students.)

Ask students to swap their completed worksheets with another student and check that everyone agrees on the spellings of the correct words.

> **Give extra support** by…
> … going through the homophones on **PPT 5 Slide 3** and giving examples of when they are used and of ways to remember them. For example, write the words 'to' and 'too' on the board, saying 'too' with great emphasis. Give the examples 'they have gone **to** the island' and then 'they were **too** late'. Ask students if they can think of ways to remember which is the correct spelling.
>
> **Give extra challenge** by…
> …asking students to think of pairs of sentences that use the different homophones on PPT Slide 3, e.g. 'Where are **your** tickets'; 'Do you know where **you're** travelling to'.

Big answer plenary	*What do you need to survive?* Ask students what they now think they would need. Ask students if they would like to be marooned on a deserted island, at least for a short time!

ADVENTURE 6

A big adventure

Assessment objectives

AO5 Communicate clearly, effectively and imaginatively, selecting and adapting tone, style and register for different forms, purposes and audiences

AO6 Use vocabulary and sentence structures for clarity, purpose and effect with accurate spelling and punctuation.

Non-exam assessment
- Silver Step component 2
- Gold Step component 2

Differentiated learning outcomes
- **Entry Level 1 students** should use some simple descriptive language.
- **Entry Level 2 students** should use appropriate words to create interest.
- **Entry Level 3 students** should choose words for variety and interest.
- **GCSE-ready students** should make adventurous and effective choice of vocabulary.

Resources
- **Worksheets**: 6.1
- **PPT 6**: Applying for an adventure

Big question — *What would your big adventure be?* Ask students what type of adventure they would like. Remind them that an adventure is an unusual, exciting or daring experience. Suggest that skydiving, mountain climbing and river rafting are adventures and ask if anyone has had these types of adventures.

Getting you thinking

Display Slide 1 from **PPT 6**. Play clip. Ask students how they felt watching the clip. Did they want to have a go themselves? Or does it not appeal? Explain to students that they are going to apply to take part in an adventure. Recap with students the types of adventures there are and include adventures that are not necessarily dangerous or extreme. Suggest that going on holiday with friends for the first time is an adventure or taking a train to a big city or a big sports match can be an adventure.

Write the types of adventures on the board as they are suggested.

> **Give extra support by...**
> ...giving an example of an adventure you would like to have.
>
> **Give extra challenge by...**
> ...asking students where they would look for an adventure holiday or simply just an adventure.

Explore the skills

Ask students if they have filled in an application form before. What was it for? What information did the application ask for? Were students aware when the form required block capitals (upper case) instead of lower case. Write examples on the board of names in lower case and upper case. Ask students to write a phrase about one of their skills in lower case, then a phrase in upper case, and then a phrase or sentence that uses both.

> **Give extra support by...**
> ...asking students if language on a form should be formal or informal. Ask them to give a sentence describing their interests in each style.

86 • Topic 1 *Adventure* • LESSON 6 © HarperCollins*Publishers* 2016

Develop the skills

Display Slide 2 of **PPT 6**. Explain to students that an application for an adventure will ask them to write about themselves, their experience and what they want to do. To make sure that they 'look good on paper', they need to use adjectives (describing words) and adverbs (to modify verbs, adjectives or other adverbs).

Refer students to Slide 2 to explain about adjectives, verbs and adverbs. Talk through a list of words and phrases that are in the context of adventure. For example, 'beautiful beach', 'sunny day', 'the group was brave', 'she was daring', 'walked carefully', 'easily swam', 'quickly jumped', 'accidentally touched', 'rarely spoke', 'fought boldly', 'lazily strolled'. Include words for Silver level that use simple descriptive language, e.g. about colour, size and emotion (for EL1), as well as words to create interest (for EL2). Write these on the board.

Put students in pairs and ask them to put the words in the correct columns under the headings of adjectives and verbs for Silver level students. Include adverbs for Gold level students.

> **Give extra support** by...
> ...creating a set of cards for students containing appropriate words for their level, to include a mixture of adjectives and verbs for Silver level students (e.g. run, go, swim, walk, race, sail; big, fun, good, great, red, happy) plus adverbs for Gold level students (as listed above). Tell students to group the words according to whether they are an adjective, verb or adverb.
>
> **Give extra challenge** by...
> ...asking students to suggest further examples of adjectives and verbs (for Silver level students) and adverbs (Gold level students).
> ...telling students to match an adjective with an adverb and write a sentence for each.

Apply the skills

Display Slide 3 from **PPT 6** and distribute **Worksheet 6.1**. Read through the adventures on the slide and tell students to choose one of them or to pick something else of their choice. Remind students about using block capitals when instructed and to use describing words when they talk about themselves.

Finally, go through EL1 and EL2 students' applications.

> **Give extra support** by...
> ...going through the form to check understanding.
>
> **Give extra challenge** by...
> ...asking students to write a covering letter to accompany their application.

Big answer plenary	What would your big adventure be? Students should now have selected an adventure in order to complete their form. Promote discussion about why they chose that adventure.

EDUCATION 1

What makes a good teacher?

Assessment objectives
AO1 Read and understand a range of texts: identify and interpret explicit and implicit information and ideas.

Non-exam assessment
- Silver Step component 2
- Gold Step component 2

Differentiated learning outcomes
- **Entry Level 1 students** should use blending to decode some familiar and unfamiliar words.
- **Entry Level 2 students** should use appropriate strategies to decode unfamiliar words.
- **Entry Level 3 students** should use a range of strategies to tackle words in a variety of texts.
- **GCSE-ready students** should use a wide range of strategies to tackle more difficult words in a variety of texts.

Resources
- **Worksheets**: 1.1, 1.2
- **PPT 1**: What makes a good teacher?

Big question — *What makes a good teacher?* Ask students whether any of them has thought about becoming a teacher. Which age group do they think would be the best to teach? Which subject might they like to teach, or would they prefer to teach all subjects to younger children? Promote a discussion about what qualities go towards making a good teacher.

Getting you thinking

Display Slide 1 of **PPT 1**. Ask students to look at the slide and go through each quality so that they understand all the words. Ask students to think of any other qualities that make a good teacher.

Ask the students, working in their groups, to pick three of the qualities and think of an occasion when a teacher they know had demonstrated each of those qualities. Check that not all groups are picking the same three. Give students 10 minutes to think about the task and then ask each group to feed back their examples of occasions.

Give extra support by...
...suggesting EL1 students concentrate on the words in the top row, while EL2 students focus on words in the second row. If students are still not sure about the word 'engaging', model an example of a bored student and an interested student.

Explore the skills

Remind students that one of the reasons why people want to be teachers is to help shape students' futures and give them the key skills they will need in order to get jobs. One of these skills is being able to read, for work and everyday life. Explain how one of the strategies they can use for reading is to decode words – this is the ability to apply knowledge of letter sound relationships, including knowledge of letter patterns, to pronounce written words correctly and figure out words they haven't seen before.

Ask students to write down the five vowels, then ask them if they can recall from prior learning the two sounds each vowel has: the short and long sounds. Model sounds for them like the short 'a' in 'apple' and the long 'a' in 'acorn'. Ask Silver level students to write down an example of each of the vowels using a short sound, while Gold level students write down a long vowel.

> **Give extra support** by…
> …modelling examples, e.g. *bit, cat, dog, bug, pen.*
>
> **Give extra challenge** by…
> …asking all students to give an example of each of the vowel sounds.

Develop the skills

Ask students the name for the letters of the alphabet other than vowels, i.e. consonants. Explain that consonants and vowels can be put together to build up words. Display Slide 2 of **PPT 1**. With EL1 students, focus on the task of building simple words with vowels and consonants. Ask them to work in pairs. Give each pair a consonant and ask them to note down as many words as they can beginning with that consonant (e.g. big, bad, bag, bat). Ask pairs to feed back their lists to the class.

If working with students at EL2 or above, explain that consonants can be put together (in 'clusters'), which build up a word and help to decode it. In these clusters, the two letters make one sound: model 'sh' for 'sheet' and 'sheep'. Explain that some words have clusters at the start of the word, while others have clusters at the end of the word. Some words even have both. In pairs, ask EL2 students to find a word or words using the initial cluster 'sh'. Ask Gold level students to find words using the initial clusters of 'fl', 'ch' and 'th'. Go round the class for students' words and write them on the board. Tell students that if another pair says their word, they have to cross it off their list.

Give students **Worksheet 1.1** and check students are clear about what they need to do. Allow 5 minutes for them to complete the tasks and then go through their answers.

> **Give extra support** by…
> …explaining that clusters are groups of things.
>
> **Give extra challenge** by…
> …asking students to find a word or words using the final clusters
> …asking students to find a word or words using both initial and final clusters.

Apply the skills

Display **Slide 3** of PPT 1. Tell students that while they can use clusters and vowel sounds to help decode a word, they should be like detectives, looking for clues of what a word means as they read it in the context of the text. Give the example of the word 'strategy'. Ask students what the word strategy could mean in the sentence: 'Our class has a strategy for raising money for our class party.'

Discuss with students the clues on the slide.

Give students **Worksheet 1.2**. Hand out an answer sheet for EL3 students to check that they have the right answers. Go through the answers with Silver level students to assess their understanding.

> **Give extra support** by…
> …giving suggested answers for 'strategy', e.g. *guess, floor, plan.* Which is correct?
>
> **Give extra challenge** by…
> …explaining that prefixes can help decode words, and asking what clue the prefixes 'pre-' and 'dis-' can give to a word, e.g. *prepare, preview, disappoint, dissatisfied.*

Big answer plenary	*What makes a good teacher?* Revisit the question and ask students whether they now have any further ideas about what skills and qualities teachers need to make them qualify as a 'good' teacher.

EDUCATION 2

What makes a good student?

Assessment objectives

AO2 Explain and comment on how writers use language and structure to achieve effects and influence readers, using relevant subject terminology to support views.

AO5 Organise information and ideas, using structural and grammatical features to support coherence and cohesion of texts.

AO6 Use vocabulary and sentence structures for clarity, purpose and effect, with accurate spelling and punctuation.

Non-exam assessment

- Silver Step component 2
- Gold Step component 2

Differentiated learning outcomes

- **Entry Level 1 students** should use some simple descriptive language when describing a student's day.
- **Entry Level 2 students** should use appropriate words to create interest when describing a student's day.
- **Entry Level 3 students** should choose words for variety and interest when describing a student's day.
- **GCSE-ready students** should make adventurous and effective choice of vocabulary when describing a student's day.

Resources

- **Worksheets**: 2.1, 2.2
- **PPT 2**: What makes a good student?

Big question — *What makes a good student?* Remind students that they started this topic by exploring what makes a good teacher. As a group, discuss whether the qualities of a good teacher are the same as those of a good student. Ask students to suggest what makes a good student and write these ideas on the board.

Getting you thinking

Display Slide 1 of **PPT 2**. Ask students to describe what they can see in the image. Explain that this is a student – Tim MacDuff. Students should arrange themselves across the classroom, with those who think Tim is a good student on the right-hand side and those who don't on the left. (The image comes from *Point Danger* by Cathy MacPhail (ISBN 978-0-00-746484-5), part of the *Read On* series.)

Read the accompanying text from *Point Danger*: *'I'm not bad, just unlucky. When something happens, I'm there and I get the blame. Somebody kicked the football through the school window. We were all playing football; I just happened to be the one who kicked the ball. See what I mean? Unlucky.'*

Ask students if any of them want to change their positions. Ask the students to explain why they have changed or stayed in the same position.

Give extra support by...
...discussing the PPT image with less confident students, exploring what events might have preceded it.

Give extra challenge by...
...asking students to judge Tim from someone else's perspective, perhaps his mother or a teacher at the school.

Explore the skills

Ask students to suggest what Tim might be able to do to make up for breaking the window and to show his teachers that he is a good student.

Distribute **Worksheet 2.1**. Students describe the measures that Tim might take in order to prove that that he is a good student.

Give extra support by…
…clarifying what each image shows and encouraging students to rehearse their descriptions verbally with a trusted adult before they write.

Give extra challenge by…
…encouraging students to use a thesaurus to select effective and adventurous vocabulary.

Develop the skills

Display Slide 2 of **PPT 2**. Discuss what each of the events could be (apologising, working hard, getting good grades, winning a prize). Ask the students to work in groups to sequence the events in an appropriate order. Encourage students to discuss their order with the rest of the class and explore any differences. Guide students to suggest either simple vocabulary (EL1), appropriate vocabulary (EL2) or adventurous vocabulary (EL3 and GCSE ready) that could be used to describe each of the events. Write the students' suggestions on the board.

Ask students to complete **Worksheet 2.2** with the order of events that the group decided on. Students should then use words or phrases (EL1), simple sentences (EL2) or paragraphs (EL3 and GCSE ready) to describe the events that occur on the day that Tim tries to prove that he is a good student. Allow 10 minutes to complete the tasks.

Give extra support by…
…reading the key words out to the students and checking their understanding.
…helping students to match words on the board to the events on the sheet before students start writing.

Give extra challenge by…
…encouraging students to incorporate vocabulary from **Worksheet 2.1** into their responses.

Apply the skills

Display Slide 3 of **PPT 2**. Ask students to work in groups to write the story they began to outline on **Worksheet 2.2**, either on sugar paper or by typing into a suitable computer program. Encourage students to use the words/phrases/sentences from their plan in their extended response.

Once the students have finished, ask them to underline/highlight simple descriptive language (EL1), appropriate vocabulary (EL2) or adventurous vocabulary (EL3 and GCSE ready), and explain to another group why they have chosen it. The other group should suggest alternatives, and together the two groups decide which one is better.

Give extra support by…
…highlighting words from students' plans that they should use in their extended writing.

Give extra challenge by…
…encouraging students to synthesise elements from the plans of several students within the group.

Big answer plenary	Ask students to reconsider the Big Question: *What makes a good student?* They should try and come up with their own responses to this question, if necessary, beginning their answers with 'Tim is / isn't a good student because…'.

EDUCATION 3

Learning in the 19th century

Assessment objectives
AO1 Read and understand a range of texts: identify and interpret explicit and implicit information and ideas.

Non-exam assessment
- Silver Step component 2
- Gold Step component 2

Differentiated learning outcomes
- **Entry Level 1 students** should recall main points from simple texts relating to Victorian education.
- **Entry Level 2 students** should recall some specific and straightforward information from texts relating to Victorian education.
- **Entry Level 3 students** should demonstrate an understanding of the main points in texts relating to Victorian education.
- **GCSE-ready students** should demonstrate a firm understanding of significant points in texts relating to Victorian education.

Resources
- **Worksheets**: 3.1, 3.2
- **PPT 3**: How is school different today?
- Copies of quiz sheet with questions and alternative answers (see 'Explore the skills)

Big question	*How cool would it be not to have to go to school?* Ask students what they would do if they didn't have to go to school. Do they think they would enjoy it? Then ask them if they would rather go to school to learn, or at the age of 10 work in a factory or on a farm for 12 hours a day, as children in the 19th century did.

Getting you thinking

Display Slide 1 from **PPT 3**. Ask students what they think schools were like 200 years ago. List students' suggestions on the board in respect of: buildings, lessons, playtime, equipment, clothing, classroom, teachers, and so on.

Play the clip. Now they have seen the clip ask students to recall any other points they saw and add to the suggestions on the board, such as discipline, dunce's hat, teacher's tone of voice and the stress on obedience.

> **Give extra support by...**
> ...showing pictures of Victorian teachers, classrooms and schoolchildren to help create an image of what it was like then.
>
> **Give extra challenge by...**
> ...telling students to write a paragraph to describe what they thought Victorian education was like.

Explore the skills

Explain to students that in those days, parents had to pay to send their children to school. Some parents, who couldn't afford to do this, paid a small amount to a 'Dame' to try and teach the children something.

Display Slide 2 of **PPT 3**. Read slowly through the text and check students' understanding. Tell students they are going to do a quick quiz to locate information. They will have one minute between questions to find the answers and write them down. First put students into small groups. Then read out the questions below. Give Silver level students a sheet with the questions on and alternative answers (see below) so that they can delete the wrong answer.

92 • Topic 2 *Education* • LESSON 3 © HarperCollins*Publishers* 2016

Questions:

1. Were 'Dame' schools run by men? yes/no
2. Was the dame a trained teacher? yes/no
3. Was the dame rich? yes/no
4. How much was the dame paid? pennies/pounds
5. What could the children learn to do? sums/sew

Give extra support by…
…telling students to look out for key words from the questions.
…giving a paragraph number to help the students find key information.

Develop the skills

Display Slide 3 of **PPT 3**. Explain to students that in their worksheet they are going to read about someone who went to school in the 19th century. To set the scene they are going to watch an interactive picture of a schoolroom in the 19th century. Show the picture (it can be found by following the link on the slide; then under 'Activities' click on 'Victorian children at work, school and play', then under 'School', click on 'Games'). As directed, move the cursor over objects that were either typical of the 19th century or not available in the 19th century.

Then ask students to recall typical objects in this era and write them on the board. Explain that the skill of being able to recall things is similar to reading a text and painting a mental picture of what they read to help them locate information.

Distribute **Worksheet 3.1**. For Silver level students, check their understanding of CVCC/CCVC and polysyllabic words. Gold level students can use a dictionary for unfamiliar words.

Give extra support by…
…reading through the text to help with blending unfamiliar words.

Apply the skills

Tell students they are now going to answer questions about the Victorian school text on **Worksheet 3.1**, which will require them to locate information and to draw their own conclusions as they did in the piece they read on the 'Dame'.

Give students **Worksheet 3.2**. Students working at Silver level can swap papers and compare answers before you check. Put Gold level students in a group to discuss their answers.

Big answer plenary	*How cool would it be not to have to go to school?* Ask students if they still think it would be cool not to go to school but to have to work on a farm or factory for 12 hours a day. Ask students what they have learned about education in the 19th century. Promote a discussion about whether there is anything that we should do in schools today that they did in the 19th century.

EDUCATION 4

School holidays

Assessment objectives

AO5 Communicate clearly, effectively and imaginatively, selecting and adapting tone, style and register for different forms, purposes and audiences.

AO6 Use vocabulary and sentence structures for clarity, purpose and effect with accurate spelling and punctuation.

Non-exam assessment

- Silver Step component 2
- Gold Step component 2

Differentiated learning outcomes

- **Entry Level 1 students** should show some awareness of full stops and capital letters.
- **Entry Level 2 students** should demarcate most sentences with full stops and capital letters.
- **Entry Level 3 students** should use capital letters, full stops and question marks accurately.
- **GCSE-ready students** should use full stops, capital letters, commas, speech marks and question marks accurately.

Resources

- **Worksheets**: 4.1
- **PPT 4**: School holidays

Big question *Are school holidays too long?* Ask students what they do in school holidays. Do they get bored during the summer weeks? Would they like there to be more terms with shorter holidays in between? Encourage a discussion and take a vote by a show of hands at the end of the discussion. Note the results on the board.

Getting you thinking

Display Slide 1 from **PPT 4**. Explain to students that the government is thinking about making the school day longer, with shorter holidays and maybe six terms a year instead of the current three. The reason why they are thinking of doing this is that in other countries that have changed to a similar sort of holiday system, students are getting better results.

Play the clip and ask students for their initial reactions. Do they think there are good reasons for looking to change the current system of holidays? Ask them to pick out one point they agree with.

Give extra support by…
… stopping the clip at intervals and checking students have understood what is being said.

Give extra challenge by…
… asking why other countries may be getting better results, e.g. more terms and shorter holidays mean less time to forget things.

Explore the skills

Give students the scenario where their head teacher has asked all students to send an email to the government to give their views on the possible changes. Explain that, for their email to be taken seriously, they need to make sure that they use correct sentence structure, grammar and punctuation. They should also include some powerful words to make their email stand out.

Working as a class, ask students for their point of view and write their comments on the board. Then put students into pairs and ask them to note down from the board three things they would like to put in their email to the government.

PPT — Display Slide 2 of **PPT 4**. Read through the text with students, focusing on the sentence structure and punctuation used, and stressing their importance, especially in a formal piece of writing. Target EL1 in sentence 1, EL2 in sentence 2, EL3 in sentence 3, and GCSE-ready students in sentence 4. Contrast writing to the government with putting a post on social media. Ask Gold level students what other punctuation they should be considering, for example commas and speech marks where appropriate.

Now ask Silver level students to write down three phrases (EL1) or three simple sentences (EL2) they can use in the email, and Gold level students to draft three sentences using the points they noted down and referring to the slide for structure and punctuation.

> **Give extra support** by…
> … helping students to select three comments from the board that they can put into phrases.
>
> **Give extra challenge** by…
> … asking students to identify connecting words other than 'and' and 'but'.

Develop the skills

Explain to students that, when they write their email, to put across their point of view more forcefully, it is good to use strong words that really show the emotion they feel. Give them the example of 'I don't like school' as opposed to 'School is absolutely horrible'. Ask them which statement is stronger and more powerful.

PPT — Display Slide 3 of **PPT 4**. Ask students to suggest words that could replace the word 'went', which appears three times. Encourage students to explain why the words are more powerful – for example, they help to conjure up a more vivid picture of the scene. If time permits, you can go on to rework the whole piece, using some of the words at the bottom of the slide.

> **Give extra support** by…
> … giving more examples of changing words, e.g. 'I like going on holiday' to 'Going on holiday is fantastic – it's awesome'.
>
> **Give extra challenge** by…
> … giving students a list of verbs (such as 'asked', 'looked', 'moved') and asking them to find more powerful verbs that could replace them.

Apply the skills

Before students write their email, discuss more powerful words to help in their writing, such as alternatives for 'bad' idea and 'good' idea. Write these on the board. Using these words, model a phrase, simple sentence and a compound sentence.

Distribute **Worksheet 4.1**, which will help them to draft their email. Remind students to correct their spelling, punctuation and grammar.

> **Give extra support** by…
> … checking students' understanding of the words in the text.
>
> **Give extra challenge** by…
> … swapping students' writing to see if they could have used more powerful words.

Big answer plenary	*Are school holidays too long?* Having heard the arguments, what are students' views now? Do they think that if school holidays were shorter, they would have less time to forget things and their results would be better? Or would they have too little rest time? Take a vote again and see whether the results have changed at all.

EDUCATION 5
A different point of view

Assessment objectives
AO3 Compare writers' ideas and perspectives.

Non-exam assessment
- Silver Step component 2
- Gold Step component 2

Differentiated learning outcomes
- **Entry Level 1 students** should identify a similarity or difference in the descriptions of an event in two simple texts.
- **Entry Level 2 students** should identify a similarity or difference between characters, events or presentation in two simple texts.
- **Entry Level 3 students** should identify similarities and differences between characters, an event, theme or presentation in two texts.
- **GCSE-ready students** should identify similarities and differences between significant ideas, themes, events and characters in two texts and make reference to the texts to support their views.

Resources
- **Worksheets**: 5.1, 5.2, 5.3
- **PPT 5**: Similarities and differences

Big question | *How can you pick out the similarities and differences in a text?* Suggest to students that it is very easy to pick out similarities and difference when you look at something. Ask them to look around the class. Who has brown eyes and brown hair and who has brown hair and blue eyes? Ask what is similar and what is different.

Getting you thinking

Display Slide 1 from **PPT 5**. Ask students to look at the slide and discuss in pairs what similarities and differences the signs have. Go round the class for answers for similarities, e.g. they are all signs for a secondary school; they all have a logo; they all say 'Welcome to'; they have telephone numbers and websites. Then ask for differences, e.g. the signs are different shapes and are in different colours; they don't all use pictures; they use different fonts (styles of writing).

Give extra support by…
… making sure students understand that a similarity is something that looks or means the same and a difference is when something looks or means something different.

Explore the skills

Explain to students that when they look for similarities and differences, they are comparing. This means they are searching for things that are either similar or different when looking at things, such as people, places, events, products, ideas. Tell students that the key to successful comparisons is to clearly identify characteristics. Explain this is a useful skill not only for reading educational texts but also for everyday life.

In small groups ask students to imagine that they are thinking of buying a laptop to do their school homework on. How would they make the decision to purchase one model rather than another one. What would they consider? Suggest price, looks, functions, weight, battery life, etc. Tell students that these are the laptop's characteristics.

Display Slide 2 of **PPT 5**. Ask students to feed back how they might arrive at a decision on which laptop to buy. Did they look at the similarities and differences? How did they compare the two? Encourage oral feedback.

Give extra support by...

... explaining to students what characteristics are. Refer to hair and eye colour.

Give extra challenge by...

... asking students to comment, in writing, on the similarities and differences, e.g. 'We know this laptop is better because..., but they both have the same...'.

Develop the skills

Tell students that they need to have an organised way of getting clues when looking for similarities and differences between two texts. Explain that using coloured highlighting pens is one good way of doing this: things that are similar can be highlighted in the same colour.

Give students **Worksheet 5.1**. Explain that they need to identify the similarities and differences in the two reports using different coloured highlighter pens.

Give extra support by...

... telling students to look for the same word used in each text on the worksheet or to look for words that have a similar meaning.

Now display Slide 3 from **PPT 5**. Explain that using a (Venn) diagram like this is another good way of organising their thoughts.

Ask students to think about the similarities and differences between two school subjects, such as maths and art/design. Replicate the slide on the board. First ask for similarities (e.g. both involve work in classrooms; both involving working individually rather than in groups). Write these points in the middle, overlapping part of the diagram. Then ask for differences and write these points in the outer shapes (e.g. maths involves more tests; art has more practical work; art can be done with different materials, not just pen and paper).

Give extra support by...

... asking questions to prompt students' answers, such as: where do you study the subject? Do you work on your own? Do you use computers?

Apply the skills

Tell students that now they have used two methods for spotting similarities and differences: highlighting texts and using a Venn diagram. They are now going to work on expressing or explaining these similarities and differences to other people.

Distribute **Worksheet 5.2** and check understanding of what is required. Give students 5–10 minutes to complete the tasks. Check students' answers.

Give extra support by...

...offering Silver level students more scaffolding in explaining similarities and differences, using people as an example: Jane and John are *similar* as they both have brown hair, but *different* because Jane's is long and John's is short.

Give extra challenge by...

...asking students working at EL2 and higher to complete **Worksheet 5.3**, which asks them to make further comparisons about school subjects.

Big answer plenary	*How can you pick out the similarities and differences in a text?* Ask students how they could now pick out similarities and differences when looking at images or video and how they would find the similarities and differences in a text (Venn diagram).

EDUCATION 6

Invitation to a school event

Assessment objectives

AO5 Communicate clearly, effectively and imaginatively, selecting and adapting tone, style and register for different forms, purposes and audiences

AO6 Use vocabulary and sentence structures for clarity, purpose and effect with accurate spelling and punctuation.

Non-exam assessment

- Silver Step component 2
- Gold Step component 2

Differentiated learning outcomes

- **Entry Level 1 students** should inconsistently match writing to structure in a simple letter about a schools sport competition and should understand words have permanence.
- **Entry Level 2 students** should show some awareness of narrative, non-narrative form and audience in a letter about a schools sport competition.
- **Entry Level 3 students** should sometimes adapt writing style to match purpose and audience in a letter about a schools sport competition.
- **GCSE-ready students** should organise writing appropriately for the purpose of the reader in a letter about a schools sport competition.

Resources

- **Worksheets**: 6.1, 6.2, 6.3
- **PPT 6**: Writing to communicate

Big question | *When did you last write a letter?* Ask students when they last wrote a letter and what it was about. Encourage answers such as replying to college places, writing thank you letters, looking for a job, etc. Ask students when they last received a letter and what it was about. Promote debate about how useful letters are now – for example, is there still a place for them now, or has social media taken over?

Getting you thinking

Display Slide 1 from **PPT 6**. Suggest to students that many people, especially younger people, aren't sure about many of the conventions of letter writing. Ask how many students *do* know the conventions by a show of hands. Refer students to the slide. Discuss with students how many of these types of letters are commonly written by email, text or social media formats. Make the point that some letters can be sent by email but are not in an email format; they are letters attached to an email.

Give extra support by...
... replicating the slide on the board and going through each type of letter. Put a tick or cross in the relevant column (email, text or social media) to make the point that letters are still important.

Give extra challenge by...
... asking students what other documents arrive in the post in letter format, e.g. grants, allowances, charity requests, job offers, bills.

Explore the skills

Give students the scenario that there is a Year 11 project to invite other schools in the area to a sports competition. Tell them that their class has been tasked with sending letters to the schools. Put students into mixed-level groups. Cut out the 'cards' on **Worksheet 6.1**, which contain the various details that should appear in a letter. Give a set of each to each group of students. Tell them to position the cards on a sheet of paper in the place they would appear in a letter. Alternatively, ask students to tell you where they should go and write them on the board.

Display Slide 2 of **PPT 6**. Tell students to check their answers against the slide. Ask groups if they got more right than they thought they would.

> **Give extra support** by…
> … telling students where the addresses go, and putting 'Dear' and 'Yours' in place.
>
> **Give extra challenge** by…
> … asking students to explain when to use 'Yours faithfully' and 'Yours sincerely'.

Develop the skills

Explain to students that there are some simple rules to follow when writing a formal letter, as opposed to an informal letter to a friend or relative.

- The address of the person sending the letter should go on the top right. Remember: 'I am always right!'
- The address of the person to whom the letter is going should be on the left.
- Underneath this address it should say 'Dear Sir or Madam' or, if you know their name, 'Dear Mr/Mrs/Ms [Smith]'.
- The main content of the letter is in paragraphs with a beginning, middle and end.
- The letter should finish with 'Yours faithfully' if you don't know the person's name or 'Yours sincerely' if you do know their name.
- The person who is sending the letter should then sign it.
- Underneath the signature is the sender's name, written out or printed clearly.

Distribute **Worksheet 6.2**. Explain to students that planning is important as it helps to give structure to what they are writing and provide a focus for the content.

> **Give extra support** by…
> … telling students that if the person is **f**aceless and you don't know anything about them it is '**f**aithfully' and that if they have a **s**urname (or name), it is '**s**incerely'.

Apply the skills

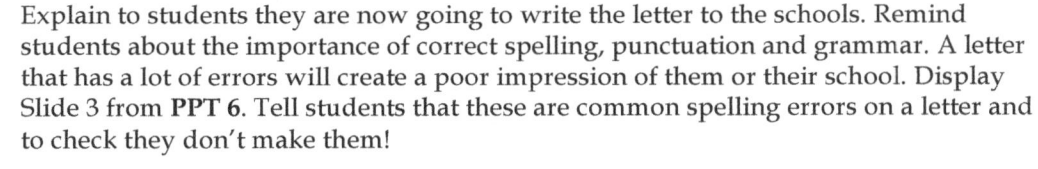

Explain to students they are now going to write the letter to the schools. Remind students about the importance of correct spelling, punctuation and grammar. A letter that has a lot of errors will create a poor impression of them or their school. Display Slide 3 from **PPT 6**. Tell students that these are common spelling errors on a letter and to check they don't make them!

Give students **Worksheet 6.3**. When everyone has finished, ask for volunteers to read out their letters. The whole class can then vote on which one to send. Depending on the mix of the group, the letters could be put on a wall for students to walk round and read. They could pick their favourite and explain why they like it.

> **Give extra support** by…
> … talking to students about what type of events might happen in a school sports competition and the type of prizes that might be awarded.
>
> **Give extra challenge** by…
> … asking students to write a letter to the schools to thank them for taking part in a successful day.

Big answer plenary	*When did you last write a letter?* Students have now written a letter, so ask them if they now have a clearer idea of the format and structure. Ask students by a show of hands how many now think that it is important to know how to write a good letter.

FASHION 1

What is fashion?

Assessment objectives

AO1 Read and understand a range of texts; identify and interpret explicit and implicit information and ideas.

Non-exam assessment
- Silver Step component 2
- Gold Step component 2

Differentiated learning outcomes

- **Entry Level 1 students** should recall the main points from simple texts about a fashion show.
- **Entry Level 2 students** should recall some specific and straightforward information from texts about a fashion show.
- **Entry Level 3 students** should demonstrate an understanding of the main points in a fashion show report.
- **GCSE-ready students** should demonstrate a firm understanding of significant points in a fashion show report.

Resources
- **Worksheets**: 1.1, 1.2
- **PPT 1**: Fashion

Big question

What is fashion? Ask students what they understand by the word 'fashion'. Is it the current designs in the shops? Clothes that you see at fashion shows? Certain trends, such as vintage? Or perhaps it is what celebrities are wearing? Ask students whether they think fashion is important. If so, do they think it is important to wear clothes that are in fashion. Promote a discussion about what clothes say about people, e.g. what wearing uniforms, suits or the latest fashion says about people and how it influences how people are perceived.

Getting you thinking

Display Slide 1 from **PPT 1**. The photo caption is at two levels so that you can choose which caption is appropriate for your students. Explain that in the world of fashion, words are often used that may be unfamiliar to them, that they do not come across in everyday life. Tell them that sometimes such words can be worked out in the context of how they are used. Explain, as an example, that a report at a fashion show might use the words on the slide. Ask how many students know what 'muslin' is. Very few, if any, of them will know what it is, but in the context of a fashion show, and through looking at the photo, they may be able to guess it is a type of material or clothing.

> **Give extra support** by…
> …explaining the word 'context', i.e. it refers to the situation, environment or surroundings. Explain that you and the students are now in a school context.

Explore the skills

Tell students there are other ways to work out what unfamiliar words mean. Give students a few minutes, in pairs, to suggest what other ways there might be to work out word meanings. Pairs can feed back to the group.

Explain to students that pictures can help put a word in context. For example, if they were asked whether they had a 'sarong' and were then shown a picture of someone wearing one – even David Beckham – they would have a clue what the word meant.

Write on the board the word 'bespoke' and tell students it is a word sometimes used in the fashion world. In pairs, give students a couple of minutes to come up with an approximate meaning or what they think the word might refer to. Ask pairs to feed back and write their answers on the board. Display Slide 2 of **PPT 1** and discuss with students how the picture would have helped them to come up with the meaning.

> **Give extra challenge** by…
> …asking Gold level students to check the meaning of the word 'bespoke' in a dictionary.
> …giving students other fashion terms to find the meaning of, e.g. 'vintage', 'retro', 'chic' and 'haute couture'.

Develop the skills

Before moving on to use the worksheets, explain to students that another way to work out what words mean is to identify the root word, a word that cannot be broken down to make another word. As an example, write on the board the word 'walk'. Explain that it is a root word as it cannot be broken down to make another word. However, by adding different endings you can make different words. Add –ed to the word on the board. Ask students for another ending to make another word for 'walk', e.g. -ing for 'walking' or –er for 'walker'.

Draw a spider diagram on the board with the word 'help' in the centre. Add suffixes around the diagram for students to make new words e.g. –er, –ed, –ful, –less, –ing..

For Gold level students, display Slide 3 from **PPT 1**. Write the numbers 1 to 8 on the board. Ask students to decide if the statements are true or false. Ask for a show of hands for each and put T or F according to the majority verdict. When completed, go through and explain whether the answer is right or wrong and why that is the case.

Now distribute **Worksheet 1.1** to all students. Tell students they are going to read about friends saying what they thought about a fashion show they had attended. Ask students to read through the text to check understanding. Students who have been looking at root words can underline any words they think are root words.

> **Give extra support** by…
> …reading the text aloud with students.
>
> **Give extra challenge** by…
> …giving students the words 'play', 'act' and 'auto' to see how many words they can make from these root words.

Apply the skills

Give students **Worksheet 1.2** to complete in conjunction with **Worksheet 1.1**. Encourage students to highlight words and phrases in the text to help them locate the relevant information. Gold level students may also find it helpful to highlight or underline key words in the questions, e.g. 'what', 'where', 'two examples'. Explain that such techniques are very useful when trying to organise thoughts about a text and to find key information. When they have finished, ask students which words they had to try to work out from their context. Ask students if there were words where a picture would have helped them to understand the word.

> **Give extra support** by…
> …working through words students found difficult to understand, to help put them into a context.

Big answer plenary	**What is fashion?** Revisit the question and see whether students have amended or expanded their views.

FASHION 2

Work wear

Assessment objectives
AO3 Compare writers' ideas and perspectives.

Non-exam assessment
- Silver Step component 2
- Gold Step component 2

Differentiated learning outcomes
- **Entry Level 1 students** should identify a similarity or difference between events in two simple texts about uniform.
- **Entry Level 2 students** should identify a similarity or difference between character and events in two simple texts about uniform.
- **Entry Level 3 students** should identify similarities and differences between character, an event, theme or presentation in two texts about uniform.
- **GCSE-ready students** should identify similarities and differences between significant ideas, themes, events and characters in two texts about uniform.

Resources
- **Worksheets**: 2.1, 2.2
- **PPT 2**: Uniforms

Big question — *Why do we have uniforms?* Start by asking students what other things, apart from fashion, may guide our choice of what to wear at home, at school and at work. Ask students whether any of them have to wear a uniform for work. Explore with them why they have one – for example, is it for safety reasons or to let customers know who they are and what their role is? Ask students whether they think that people have more trust in people in uniforms than those dressed in their own clothes.

Getting you thinking

Ask students to come up with as many jobs as they can think of for which people wear a uniform. Write the jobs on the board.

Explore with students any common factors they can find between the jobs, such as people who are in contact with the public, 'dirty' or dangerous jobs where the uniform is for protection (e.g. construction, cleaning), jobs where hygiene is important (e.g. health care), jobs where hierarchy or rank is important (police, armed services), or retail or customer service jobs where a company wants workers to be easily recognised.

Give extra support by...
...putting the jobs on the board in groupings to help with identifying a common factor.

Explore the skills

Display Slide 1 from **PPT 2**. Put students into three groups. Ask each group to look at the images and to think about as many reasons as they can why each of the people wears a uniform. Nominate one member of the group to write down their answers as a list. Give students 5–10 minutes to complete this task.

Then tell each group which person they are going to feed back on. Ask a member from each group to give their reasons why that person wears a uniform. Check with the other two groups to see whether they came up with other reasons.

Give extra support by…
…giving students a list of words and phrases to choose from, e.g. safe, clean, smart, easy to see/recognise.

Give extra challenge by…
…asking students to write a list of some of the skills required by each of the three people and then compare the lists for similarities and differences.

Develop the skills

Display Slide 2 of **PPT 2**. Discuss with students what they notice about the two uniforms – and perhaps which one they would prefer to wear – before moving on to ask students to make some formal comparisons between the two. Note similarities and differences on the board before going to show Slide 3 of **PPT 2**, which shows a Venn diagram.

Working as a whole group, fill in the Venn diagram based on the points students have made. Categories for consideration should include:

- importance of cleanliness and hygiene
- need for vital equipment, e.g. watch (for pulse-taking), phone for quick communication, weapon for protection
- handcuffs
- whether suitable for indoor/outdoor use
- importance of comfort, e.g. shoes for long hours standing up.

Give extra support by…
…offering a couple of similarities and differences to start students off, or asking direct questions based on the list above.

Give extra challenge by…
…asking students to compare the uniforms worn by people carrying out other types of job; encourage them to locate photographs of the uniforms (e.g. on the internet) and to draw a new Venn diagram comparing the uniforms.

Apply the skills

Now give students **Worksheet 2.1** and give them five minutes to read the text. Check their understanding of the text before handing out **Worksheet 2.2**. Ask students to go on and tackle the comparison tasks. Allow 15 minutes before going through to check students' answers.

Give extra support by…
…putting students in pairs to complete the tasks on **Worksheet 2.2**.

Big answer plenary	*Why do we have uniforms?* Students should be able to respond that it is to identify what jobs people do, for health and safety reasons, to look professional, etc. Ask how many of them think wearing uniforms at work is a good idea. How many disagree?

FASHION 3

What's the difference?

Assessment objectives

AO5 Communicate clearly, effectively and imaginatively, selecting and adapting tone, style and register for different forms, purposes and audiences.

AO6 Use vocabulary and sentence structures for clarity, purpose and effect with accurate spelling and punctuation.

Non-exam assessment
- Silver Step component 2
- Gold Step component 2

Differentiated learning outcomes
- **Entry Level 1 students** should inconsistently match writing to structure in an advert for a fashion store and understand that words have permanence.
- **Entry Level 2 students** should show some awareness of non-narrative form and audience in an advert for a fashion store.
- **Entry Level 3 students** should sometimes adapt writing style to match purpose and audience in an advert for a fashion store.
- **GCSE-ready students** should organise writing appropriately for the reader in an advert for a fashion store and show awareness in style for different audiences.

Resources
- **Worksheets**: 3.1, 3.2
- **PPT 3**: Purposes of texts
- Poster/leaflet promoting a fashion show and article on fashion show (see Big question)

Big question   *Why are there different types of fashion text?* Ask students what they have read or seen about fashion and clothes – for example, adverts for clothes, shops or particular brands; instructions for caring for clothes; articles about what's in fashion this season, blogs about street style. To encourage discussion, show examples of a leaflet or poster promoting a fashion show and an article on a fashion show. Ask students what the differences between them are.

Getting you thinking

Tell students that when they are reading, it is important to understand why a text has been written and what it is trying to do. They also need to think about purpose and audience when they are writing.

PPT Display Slide 1 of **PPT 3**. Then write on the board, the heading 'Purposes of text' and underneath list the words: describe, discuss, inform, instruct and persuade. Read through the texts on the slide, then ask students, in pairs, to think about what type of text is in each of the stars on the slide. Go round the class asking for suggestions and write each text on the board against its correct purpose.

Give extra support by...
...giving students other examples to help them, e.g. Instruct: how to download an app.

Give extra challenge by...
...asking students to think of other examples of each text type.

Explore the skills

PPT Display Slide 2 of **PPT 3** and read through it with the group. Explain to students that when someone writes a piece of text, for whatever reason, they have to think about why they are writing it – the purpose. This will affect the way they write it. Ask students to think of some more examples of each of the five types of text.

Then display Slide 3 of **PPT 3** and explain to students that a writer also needs to think about who they want to read it – the audience. It is also important to think about the words they use and the way they say them; this is called style. Give students the following examples of phrases and sentences. If they were making a poster to get other teenagers to come to a fashion show, which of them might they use? Which would they definitely not use?

- Great clothes
- It will be a very pleasant event.
- Strictly no adults!
- No charge will be made for admittance.
- Entry free! Just turn up.
- We would very much like you to attend.

Give extra challenge by...
...asking students how the use of formal or informal language can make a difference to who a text will appeal to.

Develop the skills

Give students **Worksheet 3.1**. Check their understanding of the different texts and ask students to spend 5 minutes matching the features and text to the type of text it is.

Give extra support by...
...helping students to match **Worksheet 3.1** with the types of text on Slide 1. Use role-play and intonation to help students understand the differences.

Give extra challenge by...
...asking students to think of examples of how a text can serve more than one purpose: for example, an advert may try to *persuade* you to buy something from a new range of clothing, but it could also have the aim of *describing* something to you, such as what is meant by 'vintage clothing'.

Apply the skills

Tell students that they are now going to produce a poster for a fashion store that has a sale on for teenage fashions. The poster is going to be put up in suitable places around the town: schools, venues, cafés, etc. As their audience is teenagers, what kind of words should they use in the poster? What is the purpose of the poster? Ask students for some phrases they might include, such as a catchy slogan. Would they use bright colours and pictures? Remind students that they want to persuade teenagers to buy their clothes, so they need to use language that would appeal to that audience.

Give students **Worksheet 3.2** and check their understanding of what is being asked. Allow them up to 15 minutes for this task. Encourage students to prepare their poster using ICT, adding images/photos, choosing suitable fonts and colours, and so on.

Once they have completed their posters, ask students working at the same level to swap their work, to see what appealed to them most and to offer any suggestions for making the advert more attractive and persuasive.

Give extra support by...
...reminding what advertisements usually do, i.e. they try to persuade you to do or buy something.

Give extra challenge by...
...asking students what other types of text there could be, e.g. argue, advise, recount, entertain or amuse, and give an example for each.

Big answer plenary	*Why are there different types of fashion text?* Students should now be able to tell you what different types of fashion texts there are and their purpose. Ask individual students for a type of text and an example.

FASHION 4
Following fashion

Assessment objectives
AO1 Read and understand a range of texts: identify and interpret explicit and implicit information and ideas.

AO2 Explain and comment on how writers use language and structure to achieve effects and influence readers.

AO6 Use vocabulary and sentence structures for clarity, purpose and effect with accurate spelling and punctuation.

Non-exam assessment
- Silver Step component 2
- Gold Step component 2

Differentiated learning outcomes
- **Entry Level 1 students** should establish the meaning of a simple word in the wider context of a simple blog about deciding what to wear.
- **Entry Level 2 students** should use contextual clues to help understand the meaning of simple words/language choices in a blog about deciding what to wear.
- **Entry Level 3 students** should identify some features of the language used by the writer in a blog about deciding what to wear.
- **GCSE-ready students** should begin to show awareness of the writer's craft in a blog about deciding what to wear.

Resources
- **Worksheets**: 4.1, 4.2
- **PPT 4**: Describing fashion
- Copies of a magazine article about fashion (one that contains plenty of adjectives)

Big question — *How important is fashion to you?* Ask students whether fashion is important to them, and why / why not. Ask students what might influence what people wear, such as school, religion, work, friends, budgets, what they see online, on TV or in magazines.

Getting you thinking

Display Slide 1 of **PPT 4**. Explain to students that the four pictures relate to different decades of the 20th century. Write on the board: 1930s, 1950s, 1970s and 1990s. Put students into pairs and give them a few minutes to decide which picture relates to which decade. Ask for a show of hands for each picture.

Now ask students to think about which decade they like the look of most and to suggest words they would use to describe the fashion of that time, e.g. cool, chic, funky, trendy, smart, classic. Discuss the words and write them on the board. Ask more confident students to talk about the decade they preferred and the words they used to describe it.

Give extra support by...
...asking students why they preferred that decade and talking through the describing words they use.

Give extra challenge by...
...giving students the words 'essential', 'vintage' and 'iconic' and asking them to write a sentence for each in relation to fashion.

Explore the skills

Explain that describing words, such as those they have been discussing, are called adjectives. Tell students that, in English, there are a lot of great words to describe clothes and through fashion they can learn a lot of new and interesting words.

Ask students to write a phrase or sentence about the clothing they like, using describing words, e.g. 'Jeans are cool' or 'I like to wear blue jeans' (Silver level) or 'I love jeans as they are very comfortable and cool' (Gold level). Then go round the class and ask more confident students what they have written. Ask the other students to say which are the describing words. Write the words on the board as students identify them. Alternatively, copy a magazine article about fashion and ask students to highlight all the describing words.

Give extra support by…
…telling students to look at the first and then second letter of the word to find it in the dictionary.
…telling students to write just a phrase describing a piece of clothing rather than a whole sentence, e.g. 'pretty dress', 'cool shirt'.

Give extra challenge by…
…asking students to think of alternative words for those highlighted in the magazine article (if used).

Develop the skills

Display Slide 2 of **PPT 4**. Ask students to look at the images and then to write one or two phrases or sentences about each of the people in respect of how they look and the clothes they are wearing, e.g. 'The girl has a cool hat', 'The man is hip' (Silver level) or 'The guy in the smart suit looks really cool', 'The girl in the long dress has lovely wavy hair', 'The red jeans are trendy' (Gold level). Silver level students should write either a phrase or a sentence, as appropriate, for each of the people in the image. Tell students they must use at least one describing word each time.

Then tell students to swap their work with another student who should identify the describing word. Allow 15 minutes for the whole activity.

Give extra support by…
…helping students to start their phrase or sentence. e.g. 'The girl in the hat…'

Give extra challenge by…
…asking students to use at least two adjectives per sentence.

Apply the skills

Give students **Worksheet 4.1**. Explain that the text is a blog. Read through with Silver level students and check their understanding. Give students **Worksheet 4.2** to use in conjunction with **Worksheet 4.1** and allow 10–15 minutes for students to complete the tasks. Remind students to use capital letters and full stops in their writing.

Display Slide 3 of **PPT 4**. Read through the examples and the four additional adjectives. Explain that the question mark represents the opposite word and ask for ideas for suitable opposites. If students are finding it difficult, give them each of the adjectives on a small card, along with suitable opposites on separate cards, for a matching exercise. Gold level students should try to write a sentence for two of the words and their opposites, as in the example.

Big answer plenary	*How important is fashion to you?* Suggest to students that now they have learnt some 'fashionable' words and described the way others look, they can now make a statement about themselves. Ask more confident students where they fit on the fashion 'spectrum'.

FASHION 5
Fashion in the 19th century

Assessment objectives

AO1 Read and understand a range of texts: identify and interpret explicit and implicit information and ideas.

Non-exam assessment
- Silver Step component 2
- Gold Step component 2

Differentiated learning outcomes
- **Entry Level 1 students** should make simple inferences and deductions about a character's feelings.
- **Entry Level 2 students** should make simple inferences and deductions sometimes supported by textual detail about a character's feelings.
- **Entry Level 3 students** should make inferences about a character's feelings based on a single piece of textual detail.
- **GCSE-ready students** should make inferences and deductions based on significant ideas, themes, events and characters.

Resources
- **Worksheets**: 5.1, 5.2
- **PPT 5**: Fashion in the 19th century

Big question | *Is fashion so different today compared to 200 ago?* Suggest to students that while there are obvious differences between clothes in the 19th and 21st centuries, there are still a lot of similarities. Ask students to suggest some similarities in respect of what we wear, e.g. dresses, shoes, coats, socks, underwear. Now ask students what some major differences might be, e.g. wearing hats all day and every day in the past, the length of skirts and dresses, women wearing trousers nowadays.

Getting you thinking

Display Slide 1 of **PPT 5**. Go back to the Big Question and ask students if there are any other similarities and differences they can see, e.g. men often wore tailcoats, ladies only wore long dresses, and so on. Then go on to ask whether they think the people shown are from the wealthier classes, and why?

Display Slide 2. Explain to students that in a famous 19th-century novel called *Pride and Prejudice*, a lot of the action takes place at a ball – the Netherfield Ball. Tell them they are going to watch a video clip created from two films based on the book and ask them to look out for how fashion has changed for going out to a special event.

Ask students to think of words that they would use to describe the images on Slide 2, e.g. pretty, handsome, silly. Write the words on the board. Explain that these words are adjectives and are used to describe something, to help paint a picture of the scene.

Give extra support by…
…telling students to focus on either the men or women in the clip.

Give extra challenge by…
…asking students if they can think why there are two distinct styles and colours of clothes for the men.

Explore the skills

Ask students what they would like to wear to a ball, a prom or a special occasion, e.g. a party or wedding. Ask all students to sketch their ideal outfit on mini whiteboards. They can add descriptions around the picture or verbally describe the outfit to a partner. Ask them to hold up their boards so they can have a look at one another's outfits. Feed back some key ideas. Allow 12–15 minutes for this activity.

Then ask students to compare the images on Slide 2 of **PPT 5** with what students had worn. What are the similarities and differences? Give students one example for a male and female, e.g. short socks under trousers rather than long socks up to the knees, a short dress rather than a long one. Use these comparisons to suggest that the actual garments are very similar, but it is just the style that has changed. Ask students why they think this is, teasing out that the function of items of clothing is still the same.

Explain to students that they have been locating information from a visual image and that this skill can also be used with text. Ask students for some examples of when they need to search texts for information. Give the example of reading clothing labels to see if a garment is hand wash, machine wash or dry clean only. In this case they are not looking for any other information apart from how to wash the item.

Develop the skills

Display Slide 3 of **PPT 5**. Explain that the image is an invitation to a ball in the 19th century, at about the same time as *Pride and Prejudice* was written. Ask students what they immediately looked for on the invitation. Was it for specific information, like the date and time? Or who sent the invite? Get a show of hands to find out who looked for specific information. Tell them this is a technique called *scanning*.

Ask which students had just glanced over the invitation to get the general idea of what the invite was for. Ask for a show of hands. Tell these students that this reading technique is called *skimming*.

Now tell students that with visual images and texts you sometimes have to look more closely, like a detective, and draw conclusions from clues in the text. This skill is called inference. Give the example that if you see someone dressed all in black, you could infer several things. For example: they may be a Goth; they may think black clothes are slimming; they may be going to a funeral.

Ask students to look at the invitation again and to work out what type of people would send this type of invitation, what their house might be like, what type of clothes they might wear. Remind students that they are making inferences, i.e. working things out from what they are observing and reading. For example, they may notice the invitation is from the 'Earl and Countess', the ball takes place in the Town Hall, the language is quite formal and 'posh' in an old-fashioned way.

> **Give extra support** by...
> ...giving students three sentences and asking them what inferences they can draw:
> - Sam looked very miserable when he got home from the football match. (Inference: Sam's team had lost.)
> - They were advised to take a waterproof jacket when they set off for their day out. (Inference: The weather forecast was for rain.)
> - Ginny left a Discount Shoes bag on the floor and is wearing new red stilettos. (Inference: Ginny had been shopping for shoes.)

Apply the skills

Give students **Worksheet 5.1**. Check understanding at Silver levels. Then hand out **Worksheet 5.2** and allow 10–15 minutes for students to complete the tasks.

Ask students to explain to a partner their final inference about the character's feelings. What evidence in the text led them to this conclusion?

Big answer plenary	*Is fashion so different today compared to 200 years ago?* Ask students for their verdict. Compare the Netherfield Ball to going to a special event today. What is the same and what is different? Whichever way students answer, ask for examples to back up their conclusion.

FASHION 6: Getting ready for a party

Assessment objectives
AO5 Organise information and ideas, using structural and grammatical features to support coherence and cohesion of texts.

AO6 Use vocabulary and sentence structures for clarity, purpose and effect, with accurate spelling and punctuation.

Non-exam assessment
- Silver Step component 2
- Gold Step component 2

Differentiated learning outcomes
- **Entry Level 1 students** should sometimes arrange ideas in appropriate order when describing getting ready for a party.
- **Entry Level 2 students** should write mainly in simple sequenced sentences when describing getting ready for a party.
- **Entry Level 3 students** should sequence ideas logically when describing getting ready for a party.
- **GCSE-ready students** should sequence ideas often in a sustained, developed and interesting way when describing getting ready for a party.

Resources
- **Worksheets**: 6.1, 6.2
- **PPT 6**: Getting ready for a party
- Sugar paper

Big question *How might you get ready for different events?* Write down a range of events (party, interview, gym session, paintball) on slips of paper and put them into a bag. Ask students to pull out an event each and explain what they would wear to be ready for each one. Discuss similarities and differences between students' responses.

Getting you thinking

Remind students that in the previous lesson, they were looking at the balls people attended in the 19th century. Ask what they remember about the balls and, in particular, what people were wearing.

Display Slide 1 of **PPT 6**. Ask students to study the picture and then draw or write at least one similarity and one difference between the two couples. Ask for suggestions and jot these on the board. Encourage students to explore what implications these differences and similarities would have on how the couples would get ready. Ask them to think about the time each couple would take and whether they would need help getting ready.

> **Give extra support by...**
> ...highlighting features on the PPT slide (e.g. woman's hair) and then asking students to describe the features on each couple in turn.
>
> **Give extra challenge by...**
> ...encouraging students to consider what other aspects of life (apart from dress) have brought about differences in the way couples get ready to attend parties.

Explore the skills

Show students a video clip of someone getting ready for a party, for example: www.youtube.com/watch?v=EHnJO_Ql78E. Discuss as a group how this is similar to or different from how they would get ready for a party. Explore potential differences between girls and boys, as well as students' opinions on whether so much preparation is necessary or appropriate.

Cut up **Worksheet 6.1** and distribute one card to each student. Explain that each card has one picture showing a stage of getting ready, as well as two words or phrases. Tell the students to pick the word or phrase that matches the picture, either by circling the correct word or crossing out the wrong word. Once they have done this, they should line up in the correct order of their events. Discuss any disagreements and explore possible alternatives.

Ask students to stick the events onto sugar paper in an appropriate order.

Give extra support by...
...suggesting inappropriate sequences of events (e.g. getting dressed before having a shower) and ask students to explain why they do not work.

Give extra challenge by...
...asking students to suggest further appropriate events that could be inserted into the sequence.

Develop the skills

Display Slide 2 of **PPT 6**. On the board, model describing the event on the slide with words and phrases (EL1), simple sentences (EL2) or extended sentences (EL3 and GCSE-ready). Ask students to describe the events they have stuck on the sugar paper in groups, making a note of any useful descriptive language.

Ask students to complete **Worksheet 6.2**, ordering the stages of getting ready to go out and then describing each of them, forming a plan for their own responses.

Encourage students to read their plans to a trusted adult (EL1), a partner (EL2) or the rest of the class (EL3 and GCSE-ready). They should discuss whether they could rearrange their events in a more appropriate order and how they could increase the clarity of their descriptions.

Give extra support by...
...encouraging students to act out the events with a trusted adult and then explain verbally what they are doing, before they write their plan.

Give extra challenge by...
...encouraging students to suggest connectives that could link the ideas together.

Apply the skills

Tell students to work individually to write up their plan into a story about someone getting ready for a party.

Once students have finished, display Slide 3 of **PPT 6**. Ask them to use a different coloured pen to number the events in their narrative. They should also check the accuracy of each other's spelling and punctuation.

Give extra support by...
...reading another student's response to them and asking them to put their finger on the page whenever they hear a different stage in getting ready.

Give extra challenge by...
...asking students to suggest more interesting vocabulary that could have an impact on the reader.

| **Big answer plenary** | Ask students to reconsider the Big Question: *How might you get ready for different events?* They should try and come up with their own responses to this question, if necessary, beginning their answers with 'Before I ... , I would ...'. |

SPORT 1: Supporting a team or person

Assessment objectives

AO1 Read and understand a range of texts: Identify and interpret explicit and implicit information and ideas.

AO8 Listen and respond appropriately to spoken language, including to questions and feedback on presentations.

Non-exam assessment

- Silver Step component 2
- Gold Step component 2

Differentiated learning outcomes

- **Entry Level 1 students** should locate some information about a sporting event from a simple text.
- **Entry Level 2 students** should locate main points and information about a sporting event.
- **Entry Level 3 students** should locate key points about a sporting event.
- **GCSE-ready students** should locate and use ideas and information, about a sporting event.

Resources

- **Worksheets**: 1.1, 1.2
- **PPT 1**: Why do people support a particular team?
- Dictionaries

Big question

How do people support a particular sportsperson or team? Ask students whether they support a team (or person, for individual sports). Ask them to discuss in pairs what has made them choose their particular team: proximity to where they live; family history; particular team members, etc. Challenge students to evaluate whether certain reasons for supporting a team may be more valid than others.

Getting you thinking

Play students the video at https://www.theguardian.com/football/video/2013/jul/24/liverpool-never-walk-alone-mcg-video Ask students to suggest any emotions that come to mind when they look at the video clip, and share the words with the class. Then ask students, in groups of three or four, to discuss occasions when their own support of a team has led them to feel strong emotion. Encourage students to ask each other about details of their memories. Students who do not support a team could talk about any occasion in their life when they have felt strong emotions.

Give extra support by…

…asking students to focus on a particular feature or image in the video clip and describe it.

Give extra challenge by…

…asking students to empathise with a supporter of a rival team – how might that supporter have felt on the occasion that they have recalled?

Explore the skills

Ask students which team or sportsperson they support. Encourage confident students to come to the front and be 'hot-seated' by the rest of the class. To guide students on what questions they could ask, first ask them if they can name five good question words? (Who, why, when, what why?) Write these on the board. Write a question for each word, e.g. Who do you support? Why do you support them? When have you seen them play/perform? Where have you been to see them? What happened? Students should note down important details from the answers given.

Next ask students to work together in groups of three or four to write down five pieces of advice they would give to someone who wants to show what a great fan they are: how should they show this? Students could focus on simple, practical details, such as what they should wear, what they might say about them to other people and how they should act if they see them live. Allow 5–7 minutes for this task.

> **Give extra support** by…
> …asking students to write some responses from the hot seating in short phrases.
>
> **Give extra challenge** by…
> …encouraging students to consider people who might have different experiences to their own, such as families with young children or fans with particular access needs.

Develop the skills

Display Slide 1 of **PPT 1**. By questioning the class, establish that these images link to the fans attending a live sports event. Ask students how these people are showing support for their team/sports personality. Then explain that one key way people show support is to watch the team or sportsperson live. Each weekend, for example, many people travel to football matches. Read through the text on **Worksheet 1.1** with the class and check understanding. Students then match the images to the text, or use words from the text to complete the gaps in the summary, as appropriate.

> **Give extra support** by…
> …supplying the line numbers for the key pieces of information that students will need to complete the summary.
>
> **Give extra challenge** by…
> …encouraging students to re-write a completed version of the summary, using their own words, but keeping the same sense.

Apply the skills

Display Slide 2 of **PPT 1**. Explain to students that they should imagine what it is like to be a fan at a big match: they have followed the travel advice and are sitting in the stands watching their team. Ask them to explain what kinds of emotions they would be feeling. Write key words up on the board.

Distribute **Worksheet 1.2**. Explain that this is an account of a match day from Lucas, a young football fan. Read the text with the class, check for understanding and then ask students to suggest how Lucas feels throughout the day. Students should use one colour to highlight any language that gives details of how Lucas travelled to the match and another colour to highlight any words that indicate the emotions he felt.

Students answer the questions about the text they have read, if possible indicating which particular details of the text have inspired their answer. Ask students to mark each other's work as you talk through the answers. Give students a few minutes to discuss whether any discrepancies between their answers are acceptable or not.

> **Give extra support** by…
> … highlighting the phrases containing key pieces of information that students need in order to answer the questions.
>
> **Give extra challenge** by…
> …prompting students to explore implicit meanings of the text in their answers, rather than simply explicit information.

| **Big answer plenary** | Ask students to reconsider the Big Question: *Why do people support a particular team?* Using the examples they have looked at in the lesson, students should be able to give at least one reason that someone other than themselves might have for supporting a particular team. |

SPORT 2: Rival supporters

Assessment objectives
AO5 Communicate clearly, effectively and imaginatively, selecting and adapting tone, style and register for different forms, purposes and audiences.

Non-exam assessment
- Silver Step component 2
- Gold Step component 2

Differentiated learning outcomes
- **Entry Level 1 students** should be able to arrange some details of an encounter with a rival fan.
- **Entry Level 2 students** should describe an encounter with a rival fan in simple sequenced sentences.
- **Entry Level 3 students** should describe an encounter with a rival fan in a logical sequence, using grammatically correct sentences.
- **GCSE-ready students** should describe an encounter with a rival fan in a sustained, developed and interesting way, using complex and compound sentences to extend meaning.

Resources
- **Worksheets**: 2.1, 2.2, 2.3
- **PPT 2**: Rival supporters
- Individual whiteboards

Big question *How would you respond to a supporter of a rival team? Discuss with students what is meant by the term 'rival'. Ask them to consider in which aspects of life you could expect to meet rivals and the extent to which these scenarios can result in conflict.*

Getting you thinking

Display Slide 1 of **PPT 2**. Using individual whiteboards, students write down as many reasons as they can come up with for thinking these people are sport fans. Less able students can draw the items in the picture that show the people support their team (the flag, hats, face paint, shirts in team colours).

Encourage students to share their responses and introduce the concept of loyalty. Through questioning of the class, develop a definition of the word and write this on the board. Give students 2–3 minutes to complete this sentence: 'As a fan of my team, I (would) show loyalty by…'

> **Give extra support** by…
> …asking less able students to write down words that describe the image of the fans from Slide 1.
>
> **Give extra challenge** by…
> …asking students to discuss whether loyalty is a universally positive attribute: challenge them to think of situations in which it might be possible to be too loyal.

Explore the skills

Distribute **Worksheet 2.1**. Explain that this is an email sent from Dave Langley, a Kingston FC fan, to his friend Alex Roberts. Kingston are one of the top teams. Alex is a fan of local team Mudchester FC, known as 'The Boggies'. Read through the text with the class and discuss Dave's attitude towards Mudchester.

The email is taken from the story *Football Fanatic*, by Steve Skidmore and Steve Barlow (Collins *Read On*, ISBN 978-0-00-746474-6).

Ask students to form groups of three or four. Allow students 5-10 minutes to write a response from Alex to Dave, defending Mudchester and explaining why he still supports them. Students can use **Worksheet 2.2** to structure their responses.

> **Give extra support** by…
> …asking students to alter words in Dave's email to change its tone from negative to positive.
>
> **Give extra challenge** by…
> …encouraging students to adopt an appropriate form and register for an informal email between friendly rivals.

Develop the skills

Display Slide 2 of **PPT 2**. Ask students to spend one minute writing down any thoughts that come into their mind when they look at the images of conflict and friendship.

Discuss how a friendship between two rival fans might involve aspects of conflict and companionship. In pairs, students should try to use the words they have come up with to describe the relationship between Alex and Dave. Allow five minutes for this.

> **Give extra support** by…
> …supplying students with key words to describe both pictures (anger, fight, argue / friend, together, happy) and ask students to come up with any similar words they know.
>
> …suggesting students try to use the words to describe some of their own relationships, rather than the fictional bond between Alex and Dave.
>
> **Give extra challenge** by…
> …asking students to look back at Dave's email to Alex and see if they can use any of the words they have come up with in this task to describe the tone of the email, supporting their points with examples from the text.

Apply the skills

Display Slide 3 of **PPT 2** and discuss with students what they think must have happened. Explain that, over the weekend, Mudchester have beaten Kingston 3–0.

Students should imagine the scene when Alex and Dave see each other for the first time at school the following Monday. Using **Worksheet 2.3**, students have to describe the scene, incorporating words from the previous task into sentences if possible.

> **Give extra support** by…
> … directing students to write a bullet-pointed list of details of the scene that might occur, then supporting them to form these into basic, unlinked sentences.
>
> **Give extra challenge** by…
> …encouraging more able students to incorporate ideas from Dave's email into their description of the scene.

| **Big answer plenary** | Ask students to reconsider the Big Question: *How would you respond to a supporter of a rival team?* Students should reflect on their descriptions of the encounter between Alex and Dave and judge whether they have behaved appropriately and realistically. They should compare the characters' behaviour with what their own response might be in a similar situation. |

SPORT 3
Making a match sound exciting

Assessment objectives

AO2 Explain and comment on how writers use language and structure to achieve effects and influence readers, using relevant subject terminology to support views.

AO8 Listen and respond appropriately to spoken language, including to questions and feedback on presentations.

Non-exam assessment
- Silver Step component 2
- Gold Step component 2

Differentiated learning outcomes
- **Entry Level 1 students** should understand the meanings of simple words in a match commentary.
- **Entry Level 2 students** should understand the meanings of most words in a match commentary.
- **Entry Level 3 students** should identify some language features in a commentary.
- **GCSE-ready students** should begin to show awareness of the effect of language features in a commentary.

Resources
- **Worksheets**: 3.1, 3.2
- **PPT 3**: How does a commentator make a match sound exciting?
- Dictionaries
- Thesauruses

Big question — *How does a commentator make a match sound exciting?* Play the class an example of sports commentary, for example: www.youtube.com/watch?v=0BdauuG8pdg. Discuss with students what the purpose of commentators is. Explore with the class what information a commentator can supply that is not immediately obvious from the visuals on television.

Getting you thinking

Ask students to suggest details that a commentator might highlight in a football match and, if possible, phrases that they might use to describe them.

Distribute **Worksheet 3.1** and ask students to complete the commentator's phrases, using the correct word types for each gap.

> **Give extra support by…**
> …suggesting events that are likely to occur in a football match (e.g. goals, red cards, substitutions). Ask students whether a commentator would describe these events in a positive or negative tone.
>
> **Give extra challenge by…**
> …asking students to suggest alternative words from the correct word class that could complete the commentator's phrases.

Explore the skills

Display Slide 1 of **PPT 3**. Explain that these are tips from football commentator Ali Cross.

Put students into groups of three. In each group, students work together to ensure they can define each of the words in Ali Cross's tips. Only if none of the group members can suggest a definition can the group refer to a dictionary.

Tell groups that you are going to read through Cross's tips and that, as a group, they must raise their hands every time you read a noun. Repeat the exercise for verbs and then for adjectives.

Give extra support by...

...highlighting two examples of each word class before starting to read the passage.

Give extra challenge by...

...challenging groups to quiz each other on the word classes of different words contained in Cross's tips.

Develop the skills

Display Slide 2 of **PPT 3**. Put students into pairs. Direct students to work together to replace the words highlighted in blue with more exciting alternatives. Allow the pairs three minutes for this.

Now combine the pairs into fours. Instruct students to discuss which of their substitutions is more exciting. Encourage students to justify their views to each other.

Each group should select the phrase they judge to be the most exciting and explain their choice to the rest of the class by completing the sentence, 'We feel this phrase is exciting because...'

Give extra support by...

...helping students to look up the highlighted words in a simple thesaurus and select appropriate alternatives.

Give extra challenge by...

...asking students to suggest an alternative to each entire phrase (rather than just the highlighted words) that would be more exciting for listeners.

Apply the skills

Display Slide 3 of **PPT 3** to show the context and distribute **Worksheet 3.2**. Read through the text with the class and check that all students understand the text. For EL3 and GCSE-ready students, check the meanings of key technical vocabulary from subheadings ('adjectives', 'exclamation marks', etc.) and explain them as necessary.

Allow students 15 minutes to answer the question: 'How does Ali Cross make his commentary exciting for the listener?'

In pairs, students share their work with each other, explaining to each other clearly which language details they have picked out to support their answers and, if possible, identifying the particular word types the commentator uses.

Give extra support by...

...directing students to explain the events referred to by the commentary in their own words, focusing on the meaning of the commentator's language, rather than its effects.

Give extra challenge by...

...ensuring more able students identify the techniques that Cross uses in his commentary to engage the listener, using the correct terminology, and that they explore the effects of these.

Big answer plenary	Ask students to reconsider the Big Question: *How does a commentator make a match sound exciting?* As students leave the room, they should be able to complete the following sentence: 'If I was a match commentator, I would say things like..., because this will make the listener feel...'

SPORT 4: The supporter's view

Assessment objectives
- AO3 Compare writers' ideas and perspectives.
- AO7 Demonstrate presentation skills.
- AO9 Use spoken English effectively in speeches and presentations.

Non-exam assessment
- Silver Step component 2
- Gold Step component 2

Differentiated learning outcomes
- **Entry Level 1 students** should identify a similarity or difference between simple match reports.
- **Entry Level 2 students** should identify a similarity or difference between characters and events in simple match reports.
- **Entry Level 3 students** should identify similarities or differences between characters and events in match reports.
- **GCSE-ready students** should identify significant similarities or differences between characters and events in match reports, supporting their views with references to texts.

Resources
- **Worksheets**: 4.1, 4.2
- **PPT 4**: Can you trust a supporter's view?

Big question | *How far can you trust a supporter's view of a match?* Ask students to imagine they have just got back from holiday. Explore how they would establish what has happened at their team's matches while they've been away. How do students judge which sources of information are trustworthy or not?

Getting you thinking

Display Slide 1 of **PPT 4**. Ask students to spend one minute thinking independently about how each of the people identified on the slide might report the event. In groups, allow students three minutes to rank the people in order of how trustworthy their accounts of the event would be. Ask students to justify their decisions.

> **Give extra support by...**
> ...asking students which details of the event they would include if they were to report it to someone else.
>
> **Give extra challenge by...**
> ...exploring the factors that might affect the people's reliability, and prompting them to discuss how far these factors may affect their group's rank order.

Explore the skills

Introduce the concept of bias to the class. Through questioning, establish a definition of the concept and write this on the board. Ask students to suggest some of the statements these witnesses may give. Write a selection of the statements on post-it notes and stick them on the board. Ask students to sort the statements on the board into those that are impartial and those that show evidence of bias. Give students three minutes to discuss their sorting of the statements and come to agreement.

Ask one pair at a time to come to the front of the class and explain why they have classified one of the statements as impartial or biased. Encourage them to use the structure, 'We feel this statement is impartial/biased because...'.

> **Give extra support by...**
> ...asking students to sort the statements into sets of fact and opinion, and then helping them to explore how those in the opinion set can exhibit bias.

Give extra challenge by...

...challenging pairs of students to suggest rewordings of the statements that would remove/introduce bias. If appropriate, you could also introduce the concept of bias through fact selection or omission.

Develop the skills

Display Slide 2 of **PPT 4**. Tell students that they show photos used in separate publications to illustrate the same match. Ask students to study the two images closely and note down any particular similarities or differences they can find. Write the following questions on the board to guide their thinking: What is going on around the players? Who is involved? Does everyone share the same expression? After four or five minutes, through questioning, share the ideas amongst the class. Ensure students add to their own ideas from others' contributions during the discussion.

Ask students to look back through the ideas they have noted down and decide which is the most significant difference and the most significant similarity. Instruct students to write two sentences, one describing the most significant similarity and one describing the most significant difference. Students should compare their work and discuss as a class which they believe is the most significant difference and similarity.

Give extra support by...
...helping students to come up with single words inspired by each picture. Once they have done this, support students to look for patterns or contrasts between the two sets of words.

Give extra challenge by...
...prompting students to explain why they believe the similarities and differences they have picked out are the most significant.

Apply the skills

Display Slide 3 of **PPT 4** and distribute **Worksheet 4.1**. Read through the text with the class and check that all students understand the descriptions of the match. Ask them to note down similarities and differences they notice between the two accounts.

Explain to students that they are going to use these similarities and differences to deliver a short presentation, comparing the two accounts. Discuss what makes a good presentation, drawing out the importance of pace, clarity, eye-contact, etc. Model a good presentation of similarities to the class and a poor presentation of the differences. Ask students to explain which of your two presentations was more effective and why.

Ask students to use **Worksheet 4.2** to plan a brief presentation of the similarities and differences they have found, replicating the positive aspects of the modelled presentation. Encourage students to present their comparisons one at a time to the rest of the class. Students should give feedback on presentation style, highlighting areas of strength and suggesting ways to further improve.

Give extra support by...
...underlining key words and phrases on **Worksheet 4.1** that indicate the tone of each match report, then supporting students to explain these to a trusted adult.

Give extra challenge by...
...encouraging students to refer to specific textual details in their presentations.

| **Big answer plenary** | Ask students to reconsider the Big Question: *How far can you trust a supporter's view of a match?* In pairs, students should explain whether the presentations they have heard have affected their views of the levels of bias exhibited by the match reports on **Worksheet 4.1**. |

SPORT 5: The perfect player

Assessment objectives

AO5 Organise information and ideas, using structural and grammatical features to support coherence and cohesion of texts.

AO8 Listen and respond appropriately to spoken language, including to questions and feedback on presentations.

Non-exam assessment
- Silver Step component 2
- Gold Step component 2

Differentiated learning outcomes

- **Entry Level 1 students** should sometimes arrange a team description in an appropriate order.
- **Entry Level 2 students** should write a description in simple sequenced sentences.
- **Entry Level 3 students** should sequence a description in a logical way.
- **GCSE-ready students** should sequence a description in a sustained, developed and interesting way.

Resources
- **Worksheets**: 5.1, 5.2, 5.3
- **PPT 5**: Making the perfect team
- Dictionaries
- Individual whiteboards

Big question: *What kind of players would make the perfect team?* Provide students with images of famous sports personalities, using sites such as: www.bbc.co.uk/sport/sports-personality. Ask students to think of other famous sports personalities who play in a team. Then ask them to describe the personality to the rest of the class, so that other students can guess who they are thinking of. Move from this into a discussion of what makes their chosen personality a good team member.

Getting you thinking

Distribute **Worksheet 5.1**. Allow students to use dictionaries to check the definitions of each of the characteristics on the sheet. Then group students into fours. Students should spend five minutes discussing which of the attributes on the sheet is desirable for a sports player.

Give extra support by...
...asking students to pick which of the words would best describe the sports personality they thought of in the previous task. Then support them to think why these attributes make their chosen personality a good team member.

Give extra challenge by...
...encouraging students to consider the potential mix of different kinds of team members: are there particular combinations of characteristics that would work well?

Explore the skills

Put students into pairs, with one of each pair sitting with their back to the board. Give these students an individual whiteboard.

Display Slide 1 of **PPT 5** and spend some time going through the players and their names, talking about why they might have been given a nickname. (Students who have read the book *Football Fanatic* should already be quite familiar with them.) Ask each student facing the board to describe one of the members of the team, if possible using some of the words from the previous task. The student facing away from the board must try to draw an impression of the team member that is being described. Allow three minutes for this task.

All now facing the board, the pairs of students should go on to assess how effective their description was. Drawing on the ideas from the previous task, discuss with the whole class whether they think the image shows an effective team or not.

Give extra support by...
...asking students to describe the players physically, rather than in terms of character. Use this as the basis of a discussion about the importance of size and strength in different sports.

Give extra challenge by...
...challenging the students describing the picture to sequence their ideas effectively, to support their partner in drawing their image with no need for corrections.

Develop the skills

Display Slide 2 of **PPT 5** and distribute **Worksheet 5.2**. Tell students that they are a football manager and the chairman of the club has suggested that the two new players shown on Slide 2 should be included in the squad. He has asked for the opinion of the manager.

Read through the descriptions of the players. Students write down their opinions of the players under the headings on the worksheet, using either phrases (Silver level students) or full sentences (Gold level students). Give students 5–10 minutes to complete this task.

Give extra support by...
...asking students to write down single words – if necessary from **Worksheet 5.1** – to describe each of the players.

Give extra challenge by...
...encouraging students to number their points to indicate how they would sequence their opinions in order to make them as persuasive as possible.

Apply the skills

Display Slide 3 of **PPT 5**. Explain to the class that both players have been brought into the team and are now playing their first match together. Hand out **Worksheet 5.3** and ask students to complete the tasks using the information given in **Worksheet 5.2**.

Ask students swap work with a partner. EL1 students should check that their answers agree. EL2 and Gold level students can read through their partner's suggestions, using a different coloured pen to underline any examples of effective detail or development.

Give extra support by...
...helping students to write words from **Worksheet 5.2** that describe a good team player, in full sentences.

Give extra challenge by...
...encouraging students to sequence their description so as to effectively build tension in their readers.

Big answer plenary	Ask students to reconsider the Big Question: *What kind of players would make the perfect team?* Discuss with students the extent to which they would consider themselves to be a valuable addition to any team, encouraging them to justify their responses by referring to characteristics they have looked at during the lesson.

| SPORT 6 | **How to be a sports writer** |

Assessment objectives

AO6 Use vocabulary and sentence structures for clarity, purpose and effect, with accurate spelling and punctuation.

Non-exam assessment
- Silver Step component 2
- Gold Step component 2

Differentiated learning outcomes
- **Entry Level 1 students** should write a narrative for a match using some simple descriptive language.
- **Entry Level 2 students** should write a narrative for a match using appropriate words to create interest.
- **Entry Level 3 students** should write a narrative for a match choosing words for variety and interest.
- **GCSE-ready students** should write a narrative for a match choosing adventurous and effective vocabulary.

Resources
- **Worksheets**: 6.1, 6.2, 6.3, 6.4
- **PPT 6**: Can you be a sports writer?
- Dictionaries

Big question — *Can you be a sports writer?* In groups, students should think back to any sports match in which they have taken part or that they have seen. Each student should explain to the rest of the group what they remember from the match. Share ideas with the rest of the class.

Getting you thinking

Before the lesson, cut up **Worksheet 6.1** and give students one word each as they enter the room. Give students three minutes to find the student who has the matching word. Once they have found the student who has their word, the students should work together to decide which word shows the correct spelling and then look up the definition in a dictionary.

Ask each pair to share their words with the class, with the rest of the students noting down the words and definition.

Give extra support by…
…encouraging students to sound their words out loud to help identify their partner quickly and identifying the correct spelling for them to reference in the dictionary.

Give extra challenge by…
…encouraging students to test each other on the spelling of the new vocabulary.

Explore the skills

Display Slide 1 of **PPT 6**. Ask students which setting would be more appropriate for the following descriptions, encouraging them to explain their ideas:

- the day your team wins promotion
- the day your team loses heavily to their local rivals
- the day you make your debut for the team you have supported since childhood.

Explain to students that setting can be used to reflect the overall tone of a narrative or description.

Students complete **Worksheet 6.2**, selecting the appropriate setting details for a triumphant match victory or a disappointing defeat. Give students three minutes to complete this task. Then ask them to compare their ideas with another member of the class.

> **Give extra support** by...
> ...asking students to write simple words ('good'/'bad' or 'happy'/'sad') next to each image.
>
> **Give extra challenge** by...
> ... asking Gold level students to write an effective descriptive sentence for each of the images.

Develop the skills

Display Slide 2 of **PPT 6** and distribute **Worksheet 6.3**. Read through the match description on the worksheet and ask students to suggest useful techniques for proofreading.

For Gold-level students only, explain that some of the errors in the description have been underlined, while others have not. Allow students 5–10 minutes to go through the text and correct any errors that they find.

> **Give extra support** by...
> ...allowing students to use a dictionary to look up correct spellings.
>
> **Give extra challenge** by...
> ...encouraging more able students to act as coaches, showing less able members of the class how to scan a text for errors.

Apply the skills

Display Slide 3 of **PPT 6**. Through class discussion, establish what events the images may signify. Students should then use **Worksheet 6.4** to describe the match. Emphasise the importance of using an appropriate setting, interesting vocabulary and accurate spelling.

Ask students to use a different-coloured pen to go back through their own work and underline any examples of new words they have used for variety.

Students then swap work with a partner, who, using a dictionary if necessary, checks that they have spelt the underlined words correctly.

> **Give extra support** by...
> ...encouraging students to describe the images on the PPT slide, rather than forming them into a coherent narrative.
>
> **Give extra challenge** by...
> ...encouraging students to use setting and vocabulary to create an engaging and consistent tone throughout their narrative.

| Big answer plenary | Ask students to reconsider the Big Question: *Can you be a sports writer?* Ask students to identify the phrase they have either used or heard in the lesson that they thought was the most effective. They should explain to each other why the phrase they have selected is engaging. |

TRANSPORT 1

Full steam ahead

Assessment objectives

AO1 Read and understand a range of texts: identify and interpret explicit and implicit information and ideas.

Non-exam assessment
- Silver Step component 2
- Gold Step component 2

Differentiated learning outcomes
- **Entry Level 1 students** should locate some points and information in a web page.
- **Entry Level 2 students** should locate main points and information in a web page.
- **Entry Level 3 students** should locate key points in a web page.
- **GCSE-ready students** should locate and use ideas and information contained within a web page.

Resources
- **Worksheets**: 1.1, 1.2
- **PPT 1**: Steam transport

Big question — *What forms of transport are still powered by steam?* Explain to students that years ago trains, boats, tractors and other forms of transport were powered by steam. Ask students if they think that there are any forms of transport that still use steam. Have they ever seen any?

Getting you thinking

Display Slide 1 of **PPT 1**. Tell students they are going to watch a video clip about the *Flying Scotsman*, a famous steam train that is still working today. (The video is interactive and students can investigate a number of aspects about the train, depending on the length of the lesson.)

Display the interactive page again. Ask students what they looked for. Did they read every detail for each clip, did they quickly look to see what would interest them or did they look for anything specific? Ask for a show of hands for each question.

Give extra support by…
…pausing the clip, and reading out and explaining the words shown on the screen under each clip.

Give extra challenge by…
…asking students to note the topics for each of the clips. Explain that these are the main points in the video.

Explore the skills

Explain to students that there are techniques that can save time when reading and help you find information quickly. Ask students what they would look for first if they received a letter about a job. Would they read it carefully through from top to bottom? Or would they start by looking for specific information, such as whether they had got the job or when the job would start? Get a show of hands to find out who would read it in the second way, looking for this specific information. Tell them this is a reading technique called *scanning*.

Ask which students would have glanced over the whole letter to get a general idea of the content, who it was from, the date it had been sent and who had sent it. Ask for a show of hands. Tell these students that this reading technique is called *skimming*.

Explain to students that there are times when it is important to read all the details of a text, and this technique is know as *reading for detail*. Ask them to give examples of when they would need to read for details, such as a letter from the bank, a job description, the contract for a job, instructions to set up a computer or electrical equipment or washing instructions on garments.

Give extra support by...
...telling students that when they look on a bus timetable for a specific bus time they use the technique of scanning. If they glance at a TV guide to see what's on, this is called skimming.

Give extra challenge by...
...asking students to give other examples of when they would use skimming and scanning, e.g. looking at book covers, recipes, train times or cinema information.

Develop the skills

Display Slide 2 of **PPT 1**. Explain to students that the slide is showing information about the *Sir Walter Scott*, the oldest steamship still in operation in Scotland. Give students fives minutes, in pairs, to look at the slide and then jot down as a bullet point list what information they have gathered. Tell them to use their own words, not to copy what is on the slide, e.g. 'What you can do: enjoy great views'.

Ask students to spend five minutes comparing information, to see whether the majority noted the same things. Then ask them how they found the information; did they use skimming or scanning?

Give extra support by...
...playing this clip to explain what a steamship is:
www.youtube.com/watch?v=OL0qWlk45mw

Give extra challenge by...
...asking what drew their attention to certain information, e.g. text size, bold print.

...asking Gold level students to read the text about the Sir Walter Scott on the website and gather more information from that (follow the link from Slide 2).

Apply the skills

Display Slide 3 of **PPT 1**. Students may find it helpful to work with a print-out of the slide. Ask students specific questions for them to find the information to answer, e.g.

- How much does it cost for an adult to go on the ship, *Lady of the Lake*?
- How long is the cruise?
- How much does it cost for a dog?

Alternatively, put students into groups and ask them to think of three questions to ask the other groups. Groups can then swap questions and answer the questions posed by another group. Allow 10 minutes for this activity.

Give students **Worksheet 1.1** and check their understanding of text. Then give them **Worksheet 1.2** and ask them to answer the questions. Allow five minutes for this.

Give extra support by...
...modelling the technique of scanning by looking for a family ticket on the Sir Walter Scott and skimming to get the general idea of what the table is about.

Give extra challenge by...
...asking students to visit the Flying Scotsman website (www.flyingscotsman.org.uk) to find out which cities it used to travel between when it was in active use.

| **Big answer plenary** | What forms of transport are still powered by steam? Students should now be able to give the answers of trains and a ship and give more information on both. |

TRANSPORT 2
A traveller's diary

Assessment objectives

AO5 Communicate clearly, effectively and imaginatively, selecting and adapting tone, style and register for different forms, purposes and audiences.

AO6 Use vocabulary and sentence structures for clarity, purpose and effect, with accurate spelling and punctuation.

Non-exam assessment
- Silver Step component 2
- Gold Step component 2

Differentiated learning outcomes
- **Entry Level 1 students** should use some simple descriptive language to write a travel diary.
- **Entry Level 2 students** should use appropriate words to create interest when writing a travel diary.
- **Entry Level 3 students** should choose words for variety and interest when writing a travel diary.
- **GCSE-ready students** should make adventurous and effective choice of vocabulary when writing a travel diary.

Resources
- **Worksheets**: 2.1, 2.2, 2.3
- **PPT 2**: City travel

Big question — *What transport would you use to get to a big city?* Ask students what means of transport they would use to travel to – and around – their nearest big city. If students say 'by car', ask what alternative they could use. Similarly, for every mode of transport they suggest, ask what alternatives there are. Explore why they would choose a certain type: is it cheaper, more regular, more convenient?

Getting you thinking

Display Slide 1 of **PPT 2**. Explain to students that the pictures show some of the ways to travel to, and travel around, a big city. Give students five minutes to discuss which of these means of transport they have been on and to describe their experience in as much detail as possible.

Tell students they are going to watch a video diary of a trip to London. Play the video clip from Slide 1 right through; then play it again and ask students to spot as many means of travelling as they can. Bus, car, coach, bicycle, boat, taxi and walking are all seen. You could also ask them if they can spot the deliberate mistake – Tower Bridge is labelled London Bridge!

Give extra support by...
...prompting students about their experience, e.g. 'When I went on a bus...'

Give extra challenge by...
...thinking of words to describe and compare the different types of transport.

Explore the skills

Explain to students that they will be looking at how to write diary entries. Ask students why they think the clip was called a travel diary. Ask students to define a diary and to give examples of the types of details that a person may want to include in a diary. Explain the importance of a chronological structure for a diary entry.

Ask students to pick three events that they would include in a diary entry about how and where they travelled to somewhere in the last week. Using paper or individual whiteboards, ask students to draw a rough sketch to represent each of these events.

This should take five to ten minutes. The class then have to guess what each other's drawings represent.

> **Give extra support** by...
> ...encouraging students to think about how they travelled to school, to the shops, cinema, etc.
>
> **Give extra challenge** by...
> ...asking students to imagine they were someone different, e.g. a celebrity, and draw the types of transport these people would use every day, e.g. plane, limousine, yacht.

Develop the skills

Display Slide 2 from **PPT 2** and read through with the students. Distribute **Worksheet 2.1**. Ask the class to read the first example of a diary entry. In pairs, allow students to discuss what is good about the diary entry and what could be improved.

Ask for students' opinions of the diary entry. Guide them to focus on the positive aspects of the text (clear sequencing, accurate simple sentences).

Now tell students to look at the second diary entry on the worksheet and ask students to discuss in pairs what the positive and negative aspects of this text are. Students' responses should this time criticise the lack of clear sequencing. Emphasise the importance of maintaining a clear chronological order in diary writing.

> **Give extra support** by...
> ...suggesting students number the sentences in the first diary entry to see how the second one differs.
>
> **Give extra challenge** by...
> ...telling students to number each sentence in the second diary entry and put them in chronological order.

Apply the skills

Display Slide 3 of **PPT 2**. Explain to students they are going to write a diary entry about a trip to London. They can use some of the words on Slide 3 to help with their writing. (EL1 students should focus on the words in column 1, EL2 the words in column 2, etc.) Remind students to write in chronological order and to use describing words to paint a picture of what happened. Give students **Worksheet 2.2**, which will help them plan their diary entry. Then give them **Worksheet 2.3** on which to write their finished entry. Allow 15 minutes for students to plan and write their diary entry.

Ask students to share their diary entries and to see if they are in chronological order.

> **Give extra support** by...
> ...talking to students about where they have been and modelling the writing with them.
>
> **Give extra challenge** by...
> ...asking students to try and find some different words for their diary that will have more impact.

| **Big answer plenary** | *What transport would you use to get to a big city?* Students should now be able to respond about the types of transport. Ask students what their preference would be and why. |

TRANSPORT 3

The long cycle ride

Assessment objectives

AO1 Read and understand a range of texts: identify and interpret explicit and implicit information and ideas.

AO2 Explain and comment on how writers use language and structure to achieve effects and influence readers, using relevant subject terminology to support views.

Non-exam assessment
- Silver Step component 2
- Gold Step component 2

Differentiated learning outcomes

- **Entry Level 1 students** should establish the meaning of a simple word in a text about a cycle ride.
- **Entry Level 2 students** should use contextual clues to help understand the meaning of simple words/language choices in a text about a cycle ride.
- **Entry Level 3 students** should identify adjectives and verbs as features of language in a text about a cycle ride.
- **GCSE-ready students** should identify words or phrases that create atmosphere or build character in a text about a cycle ride.

Resources
- **Worksheets**: 3.1, 3.2
- **PPT 3**: The long cycle ride

Big question — *Could you ride from John O'Groats to Land's End?* Ask students if they have heard about this challenging cycle ride. Explain that it is riding from one end of the UK to the other (if possible, show it on a map of Great Britain). Explain that some people do it in a week, while others take several weeks. Some people do it as a charity ride; others just want to challenge themselves.

Getting you thinking

Display Slide 1 of **PPT 3**. Tell students they are going to watch a clip about this challenge to set the scene. After playing the clip, ask students if they think they might be up to such a challenge. In pairs, ask students to come up with words that could describe how the cyclists might feel on the journey.

Give extra support by…
…giving students a couple of words that might describe what the challenge is like, e.g. tiring, hard. Remind them these are adjectives, which are describing words.

Give extra challenge by…
…asking students to give three adjectives and three verbs that might describe this challenge.

Explore the skills

Display Slide 2 or 3 of **PPT 3**. Slide 2 is intended for Silver level students and Slide 3 for Gold level. Explain that there are words and phrases in the extract that describe how the cyclist was feeling about the challenge. These are highlighted in blue. Ask students to suggest what these words and phrases tell us about the cyclist's feelings.

Ask students if they can explain what the phrase in red means (as strong as an ox). All students should be able to discuss this and make suggestions. Gold level students may know it is a simile – for more on this, they can go on the internet to http://examples.yourdictionary.com/examples-of-similes.html

Tell groups you are going to read the extract aloud and that they should raise their hands every time you read a naming word/noun. Then repeat the exercise with describing words/adjectives and with doing words/verbs.

> **Give extra support by...**
> ...highlighting two examples of each word class before starting to read the extract.
>
> **Give extra challenge by...**
> ...telling students to identify all the nouns, verbs, adjectives and connectives on the slide. They should put them under each heading and then swap with students of similar ability to see if they agree.

Develop the skills

Display Slide 4 (Silver level) or 5 (Gold level) of **PPT 3**. Put students in pairs and ask them to replace the words highlighted in red with more exciting alternatives. Some possibilities are suggested on Slide 4.

> **Give extra support by...**
> ...reading the text with students and discussing each red word to help them find appropriate alternatives.
>
> **Give extra challenge by...**
> ...telling students to revisit http://examples.yourdictionary.com/examples-of-similes.html to find similes that would work with the sentences.

Now combine the pairs into fours. Ask students to discuss which of their alternative word(s) is more exciting. Encourage students to justify their views to each other.

Each group should select the word or phrase they think is the most exciting and explain their choice to the rest of the class by completing the sentence, 'We feel this word/phrase is more exciting because...'.

Give students **Worksheet 3.1**. Read through the text with the students as necessary and check their understanding of the vocabulary. For Gold level students, double-check the meanings of key technical terms such as adjectives, nouns and verbs.

Apply the skills

Explain to students that by changing words and using different phrases as they have been doing in the lesson, they can make a text more interesting. This is part of the way a writer can use language for effect, creating pictures in the reader's mind and helping them to understand what is being written.

Give students **Worksheet 3.2** and tell them to refer back to **Worksheet 3.1** if they are not sure about any meanings. Gold level students can rewrite the story by changing as many words and phrases as they can.

> **Give extra challenge by...**
> ...asking EL3 and GCSE-ready students to write a completely different story based on a long cycle ride.

Big answer plenary	*Could you ride from John O'Groats to Land's End?* Ask students the question again and then ask them to explain/describe why they would or wouldn't like to do it.

TRANSPORT 4

Flying high

Assessment objectives

AO5 Organise information and ideas, using structural and grammatical features to support coherence and cohesion of texts.

Non-exam assessment
- Silver Step component 2
- Gold Step component 2

Differentiated learning outcomes
- **Entry Level 1 students** should sometimes arrange ideas in appropriate order by sequencing three related events in a picture-based story.
- **Entry Level 2 students** should write a story mainly in simple sequenced sentences, making links between ideas or events.
- **Entry Level 3 students** should sequence ideas in a story logically with a clear beginning, middle and end.
- **GCSE-ready students** should sequence ideas often in a sustained, developed and interesting way, including paragraphing when writing a story.

Resources
- **Worksheets**: 4.1, 4.2, 4.3
- **PPT 4**: Helicopters

Big question — *What is it like flying in a helicopter?* Ask if any students have ever had the experience of flying in a helicopter. If so, ask them to tell the class about it. If not, ask students what they think it would be like, e.g. cool, noisy, exciting, scary.

Getting you thinking

Display Slide 1 from **PPT 4**. Tell students they are going to watch a clip about helicopters. Play the clip and stop after 2:04 minutes. Ask students to discuss in pairs who they think might use a helicopter, e.g. police, fire fighters, paramedics, army, business people, celebrities, tourists. Then take ideas from pairs, writing the roles on the board.

Give extra support by…
…suggesting who might use a helicopter and asking for a show of hands from students who agree with your suggestion.

Give extra challenge by…
…asking students to write the roles on sticky notes with accurate spelling.

Explore the skills

Explain that helicopter rides can be vital because helicopters can fly and land in places that other forms of transport find difficult to reach. However, pilots must be very skilful indeed and they face many challenges when they fly helicopters. Go on to say that accounts of helicopter rides would make good stories for this reason. Then elicit from students what makes a good story. Is it:

- when everything goes well and nothing interesting happens? (No)
- when a person faces a challenge or change in their life? (Yes)

Give extra support by…
…giving a simple example of a well-known story such as James Bond but in which nothing happens! (James Bond is flying a helicopter and suddenly… lands safely!).

Give extra challenge by…
…asking students to think of any story they have read or seen recently in which a character faces a challenge or problem.

Now look at Slide 2 of **PPT 4**. This shows a sequence of events. Ask students to discuss what is happening in the story. Remind them that most stories tell us about someone who faces a problem or challenge and whether they can deal with it.

Develop the skills

Explain that stories must be clear and easy to follow, so the events must be put in an order that makes sense. Give out **Worksheet 4.1**. This deals with sequencing of ideas for stories and completing a given structure. Students can work in pairs to begin with, or more confident students may be able to complete the work on their own. Allow 10 minutes for this activity. Check understanding of all vocabulary.

Once they have completed their work, elicit the key idea that all stories have a structure – a beginning, middle and end – but that each part of the story does a different thing and we need to be clear about what that is. Ask each level of students (EL1, 2 and 3) to briefly report back on what they had to do. Ask students from EL2 and EL3 to read out their completed stories, or read selected ones out yourself.

Explain that creating a story with events in an order that makes sense is just the first step; it is also important to choose words that help the reader. Display Slide 3 of **PPT 4**. This shows a simple paragraph from another helicopter story. Read the paragraph out and ask for a show of hands from anyone who can spot what is wrong with it. Elicit the idea that the problem is in the use of the verbs. Some are in the present ('looks', 'have' – as if things are happening now) and some are in the past ('cried', 'were', 'died' – things that have already happened). We call this the tense. It is not vital for students to know this word, but they do need to understand that sticking to the same tense for something that happens in a story helps it make sense.

> **Give extra support** by…
> …pointing out that it is not the story (the ideas) that are wrong, but something to do with the way the words are written.
>
> **Give extra challenge** by…
> …asking students to suggest the alternative verbs to make them all present tense, or all past tense.

Display Slide 4 of **PPT 4**. Explain that most stories use the past tense verbs, so 'cried', 'were' and 'died'. The correct version of the story can be read aloud with the verbs in bold. Elicit how the verbs 'looks', and 'have' have been changed to the past tense.

Apply the skills

Display Slide 5 of **PPT 4** and read it aloud to students. Tell students they are going to write a short story, in their own words, about a ride in a helicopter. Explain that they all have the same facts to start with. Give students **Worksheet 4.2** and ask them to plan/draw their story. Students working at EL1 can then add words and phrases; EL2 students can add simple sentences; EL3 students can add sentences; GCSE-ready can use compound and complex sentences to develop paragraphs within their story. EL3 and GCSE-ready should write their story on **Worksheet 4.3**.

> **Give extra support** by…
> …modelling the sentences they could write in their story.
>
> **Give extra challenge** by…
> …asking some students to add supplementary paragraphs to provide more detail.

Big answer plenary	*What is it like flying in a helicopter?* Silver level students should now understand the basic structure of a story; Gold level students should be able to write clear sentences with mostly consistent verbs suitable for each part of the story.

TRANSPORT 5: Travelling to France

Assessment objectives

AO5 Communicate clearly, effectively and imaginatively, selecting and adapting tone, style and register for different forms, purposes and audiences.

AO6 Use vocabulary and sentence structures for clarity, purpose and effect with accurate spelling and punctuation.

Non-exam assessment
- Silver Step component 2
- Gold Step component 2

Differentiated learning outcomes

- **Entry Level 1 students** inconsistently match writing to structure and understand words have permanence in response to a blog.
- **Entry Level 2 students** should show some awareness of narrative, non-narrative form and audience when responding to a blog.
- **Entry Level 3 students** should sometimes adapt writing style to match purpose and audience when responding to and writing blogs.
- **GCSE-ready students** should organise writing appropriately for the purpose of the reader when responding to and writing blogs.

Resources
- **Worksheets**: 5.1, 5.2, 5.3
- **PPT 5**: Travelling to France

Big question *What are the different ways to get to France?* Start by asking students what they know about France and its location in relation to the UK. Then ask students whether any of them have been to France? How did they get there and what did they see? Who did they go with?

Getting you thinking

Show students Slide 1 of **PPT 5**. Then ask students to work in pairs or small groups to elicit what they know about France.

Hand out **Worksheet 5.1**, which they should use as the basis for their discussion. The worksheet can be printed at A3 size and completed by all groups.

Take feedback and complete a composite grid on the board. Then follow up with further questions specifically related to transport. Promote a discussion about car, ferry, plane, coach and Eurostar. Which do they think would be cheapest, quickest, easiest, most comfortable, etc?

Ask students what words they know in French. Explain to students that, whatever the language, it is important to know the difference between writing something formally or informally. Explain that in written text such as an email, 'Cheers' is an informal way of saying 'Thank you' or 'Goodbye'. Explain that formal means polite language you might use with people you do not know very well or when you want to show respect to someone (e.g. a schoolteacher, work colleague or older person). Informal means language you might use when chatting with friends or in writing to people you know well.

> **Give extra support by...**
> ...asking students how they would say 'Goodbye' to their friends?
>
> **Give extra challenge by...**
> ...asking students to rank these forms of 'goodbye' on a scale of informality to formality: 'Goodbye', 'Laters!', 'See you', 'Ciao!', 'Bye'.

Explore the skills

Stress to students once again the importance of being able to know the difference between the types of words they should use when addressing different people in writing. For example, a student wouldn't write a letter to a tutor and start it 'Hiya mate' or send an email to a close friend starting it with 'Dear Miss Bell'. Explain that the language they use will depend on the reason they are writing something: a letter applying for a job will need very different language compared to a post on a social media site about a night out.

Display Slide 2 of **PPT 5**. In pairs ask students to think of the formal word for each of the words listed on the slide. After five minutes, ask for suggestions. Then display Slide 3 of **PPT 5** to show the more formal versions of each of the words.

> **Give extra support** by…
> …creating a set of cards containing all the words on Slides 2 and 3 of **PPT 5** and giving out one card to each student; the students then have to pair up by finding the student with the corresponding formal or informal word.
>
> **Give extra challenge** by…
> …asking students to write three formal sentences using each of the words children, money and fashionable and three informal sentences with equivalent words.

Develop the skills

Explain to students that as well as knowing the difference between formal and informal language, they also need to know when to use it.

Display Slide 4 from **PPT 5**. Put students into pairs and ask them to look at each example on the slide and say for each number if the language should be formal or informal.

> **Give extra support** by…
> …eliciting from students what the form is (tweet, letter, etc.), who the audience is, and what the purpose is in each case. Apply what they know about how language is generally used in these forms and for these purposes.
>
> **Give extra challenge** by…
> …asking students about occasions when they have used informal language when formal language would have been more appropriate.

Apply the skills

Now give students **Worksheet 5.2**. Check that all students understand the text before distributing **Worksheet 5.3**. Allow 15 minutes to complete the activity.

> **Give extra support** by…
> …talking through each type of communication to give clues if formal or informal.
>
> **Give extra challenge** by…
> …telling students to turn the formal sentences into informal and vice-versa.

Big answer plenary	*What are the different ways to get to France?* Students should now be able to list the various methods: car, ferry, coach, plane and Eurostar. They should also be able to say which they prefer and explain why.

TRANSPORT 6

Cars in the future

Assessment objectives

AO5 Communicate clearly, effectively and imaginatively, selecting and adapting tone, style and register for different forms, purposes and audiences.

AO6 Use vocabulary and sentence structures for clarity, purpose and effect with accurate spelling and punctuation.

Non-exam assessment
- Silver Step component 2
- Gold Step component 2

Differentiated learning outcomes
- **Entry Level 1 students** should show some awareness of full stops and capital letters in texts about cars.
- **Entry Level 2 students** should demarcate most sentences with full stops and capital letters in texts about cars.
- **Entry Level 3 students** should use capital letters, full stops and question marks usually accurately in texts about cars.
- **GCSE-ready students** should use full stops, capital letters, commas, speech marks and question marks accurately, and begin to use punctuation within sentences in texts about cars.

Resources
- **Worksheets**: 6.1, 6.2
- **PPT 6**: Cars in the future

Big question — *What will we be driving in 50 years time?* Ask students what they think might be the answer to that question. Encourage discussion about driverless cars and lorries that are currently being trialled. Suggest we may be 'flying' round the streets in 'hover cars'. Do they think that is possible?

Getting you thinking

Display Slide 1 from **PPT 6**. Tell students they are going to look at what cars might look like in the future. Play the clip for at least two minutes. Then, use a speaking and listening frame (see Appendix 1) to encourage a discussion about which cars students liked and what they thought would happen to cars over the next ten years. (Ask students: Which cars from the clip did you like best? Did you notice anything in particular about the designs? How do you think cars will change over the next ten years?)

Ask students what the people who design cars need to be able to do in addition to their obvious design and engineering skills, e.g. write legibly, spell words correctly and put their ideas down in writing. Suggest to students that some of the designs might go wrong if they couldn't do that.

> **Give extra support** by...
> ...explaining 'legibly' and stressing the importance of using upper and lower case letters correctly.
>
> **Give extra challenge** by...
> ...asking what other skills car designers might need, e.g. maths, drawing.

Explore the skills

Go through the rules about when to use capital letters, full stops and question marks. Next tell students they are now going to pretend to be the boss of a big car company. They have received a report from one of their designers, but it has some mistakes in the use of capital letters and punctuation. Their job is to correct the sentences.

Give out **Worksheet 6.1**. Ask students to work individually to find the errors and then write the correct sentences underneath. Allow 6–8 minutes for the activity.

Ask students to swap with another student for them to check the use of punctuation and capital letters. Do they both agree? Did they use capital letters at the start of each sentence?

> **Give extra support** by…
> …providing clues for each sentence, e.g. how many errors and what sort.
>
> **Give extra challenge** by…
> …writing another sentence in the report about the company's new cars. It could mention a simple design feature such as the colour or number of doors.

Develop the skills

Display Slides 2 and/or 3 of **PPT 6** (Slide 2 is suitable for Silver level students; Slide 3 is suitable for EL3 & GCSE-ready students). Explain to students that sometimes spelling mistakes can be amusing or create problems. With road signs if you cannot read what they say, then you might make a mistake. Ask students to look at these signs and work out what the mistake is. They should then make a note of what they think the correct spelling should be.

Allow five minutes for this activity. Then ask students to feed back, saying what the mistakes are on the road signs and offering the correct spellings.

> **Give extra support** by…
> …printing out the slides for clarity if required.
>
> **Give extra challenge** by…
> …asking students to come up with two or three correctly-spelt road signs of their own, e.g. to warn about roadworks, an accident or cattle on the motorway.

Apply the skills

Display Slide 4 from **PPT 6**. Tell students they are going to write about what features they would like their car to have and what is good about it. Give out **Worksheet 6.2**. Give students 10–15 minutes for their writing. Ask more confident students to read their piece aloud.

> **Give extra support** by…
> …modelling the first sentence on the worksheet, and drawing attention to capital letters and relevant punctuation as you do so.
>
> **Give extra challenge** by…
> …asking students to swap their work to check for legibility, spelling and punctuation.

Big answer plenary	*What will we be driving in 50 years time?* Ask students to give a description of what car they think they will be driving and ask what power they think it will use.

Component 2
Creative Writing & Reading

© HarperCollins*Publishers* 2016 — Topic 5 *Transport* • LESSON 6 • 135

EL1 Silver | **Group discussion support frame**

Agree

I agree.

That is a good idea.

I think so too.

I like your idea.

Disagree

I disagree. I think...

I do not agree with that.

That is a good idea, but...

I am not sure.

Connectives

... because ...

... and ...

++ ... also ...

... but ...

Listen

Look at the speaker.

Let the speaker finish.

Help the speaker by smiling  and nodding.

Appendix 1

136 • Spoken language support frames

© HarperCollins*Publishers* 2016

EL2 & EL3 Group discussion support frame

Agree	Disagree
• I agree. • That's a good idea. • I think so too. • I like your idea.	• That's an interesting idea but... • I disagree. I think... • I don't agree with that. • Yes, but what if... • I'm not sure.
Connectives	**Listen**
• ... because ... • ... and ... • ... also ... • ... but ... • ... however ...	• Look in the direction of the speaker. • Let the speaker finish what they are saying. • Encourage the speaker for example by smiling, nodding, leaning towards them.

EL1 Silver — **Presentation support frame**

Present

- Look at your listeners.
- Speak slowly.
- Smile.

Listen

- Look at the speaker.
- Let the speaker finish.
- Help the speaker by smiling and nodding.

Ask questions

- Tell us more about…

EL2 & EL3 — **Presentation support frame**

Presenting:

- Look at your audience.
- Smile.
- Use Standard English.
- Vary your tone, pace, volume and intonation.
- Use gestures to support what you're saying.

Listening:

- Look at the speaker.
- Let the speaker finish what they are saying.
- Help the speaker by smiling, nodding and leaning towards them.

Asking questions:

- 'Could you tell us more about…?'
- 'What did you mean when you said…?'

EL1/2 Silver — Self-assessment sheet

Name: .... Topic: ....

Lesson 1 target	How do you feel about the skills in today's lesson?
	☐ I met my target. ☐ I met my target with help. ☐ I need to work on my target.

Lesson 2 target	How do you feel about the skills in today's lesson?
	☐ I met my target. ☐ I met my target with help. ☐ I need to work on my target.

Lesson 3 target	How do you feel about the skills in today's lesson?
	☐ I met my target. ☐ I met my target with help. ☐ I need to work on my target.

Lesson 4 target	How do you feel about the skills in today's lesson?
	☐ I met my target. ☐ I met my target with help. ☐ I need to work on my target.

Lesson 5 target	How do you feel about the skills in today's lesson?
	☐ I met my target. ☐ I met my target with help. ☐ I need to work on my target.

Lesson 6 target	How do you feel about the skills in today's lesson?
	☐ I met my target. ☐ I met my target with help. ☐ I need to work on my target.

Appendix 2

EL3 Gold — Self-assessment sheet

Name: .... **Topic:** ....

Lesson 1 target	Achieved? (Y, P, N)	Evidence

One way I can improve my learning next time is:

Lesson 2 target	Achieved? (Y, P, N)	Evidence

One way I can improve my learning next time is:

Lesson 3 target	Achieved? (Y, P, N)	Evidence

One way I can improve my learning next time is:

EL3 Gold — Self-assessment sheet

Name: .... **Topic:** ....

Lesson 4 target	Achieved? (Y, P, N)	Evidence
One way I can improve my learning next time is:		

Lesson 5 target	Achieved? (Y, P, N)	Evidence
One way I can improve my learning next time is:		

Lesson 6 target	Achieved? (Y, P, N)	Evidence
One way I can improve my learning next time is:		

Appendix 2

Acknowledgements

The publishers gratefully acknowledge the permission granted to reproduce copyright material in the worksheets and PPT slides accompanying this book. Every effort has been made to contact the holders of copyright material, but if any have been inadvertently overlooked, the publisher will be pleased to make the necessary arrangements at the first opportunity.

Illustrations: t = top, c = centre, b = bottom, r = right, l = left, SS = Shutterstock.com

Celebrities

1.1 EL1/2/3: Syda Productions/SS (t), kak2s/SS (c), dwphotos/SS (b), **2.1 EL1/2:** Dennis Makarenko/SS (r2), Tania Sohlman/SS (r3), dwphotos/SS (r4), **3.1 EL1:** michaeljung/SS (tl), Phovoir/SS (tc), Monkey Business Images/SS (tr), Zurijeta/SS (bl), Monkey Business Images/SS (bc), Monkey Business Images/SS (br), **3.1 EL3:** michaeljung/SS (c), **3.2 EL1:** Zurijeta/SS (l1), Everett Historical/SS (l2), Everett Historical/SS (r1), Everett Historical/SS (r2), Zoom Team/SS (r3), **3.2 EL2/3:** Everett Historical/SS (r1), **4.1 EL1:** Jeka/SS (r1), superjoseph/SS (r2), © epa european pressphoto agency b.v. / Alamy Stock Photo (r3), Featureflash Photo Agency/SS (r4), Claudio Divizia/SS (r6), **4.1 EL2/3:** © epa european pressphoto agency b.v. / Alamy Stock Photo (l1), Featureflash Photo Agency/SS (l2), **4.2 EL1:** Featureflash Photo Agency/SS (r1), Claudio Divizia/SS (r3), Jeka/SS (r4), superjoseph/SS (r5), © epa european pressphoto agency b.v. / Alamy Stock Photo (r6), **4.3 EL1:** Monkey Business Images/SS (r1), aslysun/SS (r2), Zurijeta/SS (r3), Volt Collection/SS (r4), superjoseph/SS (r5), murphy81/SS (l2), bikeriderlondon/SS (l3), Alexander Korobov/SS (l4), Claudio Divizia/SS (l5), **5.1 EL1:** Stuart Miles/SS (r1), ColinCramm/SS (r2), ColinCramm/SS (r3), Viktorija Reuta/SS (r4), **5.2 EL1:** Elena Runova/SS (t1), Marushchak Olha/SS (t2), larryrains/SS (t3), BeRad/SS (t4), Makkuro GL/SS (t5), grmarc/SS (t6), Bruno Ismael Silva Alves/SS (r1), Konstantin L/SS (r2), Andre tiyk/SS (r3), Amy Johansson/SS (r4), **5.2 EL2:** Bruno Ismael Silva Alves/SS (r1), Konstantin L/SS (r2), Andre tiyk/SS (r3), Amy Johansson/SS (r4), **5.3 EL1:** Elena Runova/SS (t1), Marushchak Olha/SS (t2), larryrains/SS (t3), BeRad/SS (t4), Makkuro GL/SS (t5), grmarc/SS (t6), Brian Goff/SS (t7), **6.1 EL1:** Andrea Raffin/SS (t), dwphotos/SS (t2), Yeko Photo Studio/SS (r4), Maridav/SS (r7), **6.1 EL2/3:** Andrea Raffin/SS (t), **6.2 EL1/2:** Halfbottle/SS (tl1), Dennis Makarenko/SS (tl2), Yeko Photo Studio/SS (tr1), Yuriy Kulik/SS (tr2), Maridav/SS (b1), Halfbottle/SS (b2), Maridav/SS (b3), ostill/SS (b4), Axel Bueckert/SS (b5), **6.3 EL1:** Dennis Makarenko/SS (t1), bikeriderlondon/SS (t2), 1000 Words/SS (t3), dwphotos/SS (t4), larryrains/SS (b2), **PPT 1:** Syda Productions/SS (1t), bioraven/SS (1b), zaniman/SS (3l), Syda Productions/SS (3r), **PPT 2:** kak2s/SS (1tr), AMA/SS (1cl), Sean Liew/SS (1c), dwphotos/SS (1cr), Dennis Makarenko/SS (1bl), Tania Sohlman/SS (1br), kak2s/SS (2tr), Denis Makarenko/SS (2cr), Tania Sohlman/SS (2bl), dwphotos/SS (2br), kak2s/SS (3tr), dwphotos/SS (3cl), Tania Sohlman/SS (3bl), Denis Makarenko/SS (3br), **PPT 3:** michaeljung/SS (1l), Everett Historical/SS (2r), Volt Collection/SS (3l), Everett Historical/SS (3r), **PPT 4:** 360b/SS (1l), JStone/SS (1c), AHMAD FAIZAL YAHYA/SS (1tr), Featureflash Photo Agency/SS (1br), JStone/SS (2l), Featureflash Photo Agency/SS (2r), JStone/SS (3l), Featureflash Photo Agency/SS (3r), **PPT 5:** bioraven/SS (1c), AMA/SS (2r), AMA/SS (3t), Denis Makarenko/SS (3b), sniegirova mariia/SS (4b), **PPT 6:** Denis Makarenko/SS (2t), bikeriderlondon/SS (2b), bikeriderlondon/SS (3c)

Detectives

1.1a EL1: jijomathaidesigners/SS (l1), Lybimkavector/SS (l2), stockshoppe/SS (l3), artbesouro/SS (l4), ArtMari/SS (c), VikaSukh/SS (r1), Photobac/SS (r2), **1.1b EL1:** Talashow/SS (l1), Talashow/SS (l2), Photobac/SS (l3), Hannes Thirion/SS (l4), 1000 Words/SS (r2), Claudio Divizia/SS (r4), **1.1b EL2:** 1000 Words/SS (r1), Photobac/SS (r2), Hannes Thirion/SS (b1), Claudio Divizia/SS (b2), **1.2 EL1:** Miguel Angel Salinas Salinas/SS (l1), Siberica/SS (c2), Kluva/SS (c3), Svetlana Ivanova/SS (r1), **2.2 EL1:** zig8/SS (t2), Kluva/SS (t3), **2.3 EL1:** Kluva/SS (r5), **3.2b EL1:** Tribalium/SS (c), elmm/SS (b), **4.1 EL1:** dedMazay/SS (r1), Ralf Juergen Kraft/SS (r2), Ariros/SS (r3), Mike Rosskothen/SS (r4), **4.1 EL2/3:** dedMazay/SS (l1), Ariros/SS (l2), Ralf Juergen Kraft/SS (r1), Mike Rosskothen/SS (r2), **4.2 EL1:** Mike Rosskothen/SS (r3), Strejman/SS (r4), Ariros/SS (r5), **4.2a EL2:** Strejman/SS (c), Ralf Juergen Kraft/SS (b), **5.1 EL1:** boonchoke/SS (tr), De-V/SS (tc), Unuchko Veronika/SS (tb), boonchoke/SS (b1), Unuchko Veronika/SS (b2), De-V/SS (b3), **5.1a EL2:** boonchoke/SS (t), De-V/SS (c), Unuchko Veronika/SS (b), **6.1 EL1/2:** Oleg Golovnev/SS (l3), dusan.dada/SS (l4), **6.2 EL1:** ostill/SS (l1), AVN Photo Lab/SS (l2), Anthony Hall/SS (l3), Olga Popova/SS (r3) **PPT 1:** ostill/SS (1r), Fer Gregory/SS (2b), Andrey Burmakin/SS (3r), **PPT 2:** Minerva Studio/SS (1tr), KieferPix/SS (1bl), puhhha/SS (1bc), **PPT 3:** elmm/SS (1r), Ints Vikmanis/SS (2l), **PPT 4:** rkl_foto/SS (1t), joloei/SS (1bl), Nick Hawkes (1br), Ralf Juergen Kraft/SS (2l), Ad Meskens/SS (br), **PPT 5:** Ingaga/SS (1tr), Lane V. Erickson/SS (1cl), elnavegante/SS (1bl), Brian A Jackson/SS (1br), Picsfive/SS (2c), **PPT 6:** ostill/SS (1l), Olga Popova/SS (2r)

Exhibitions

1.1 EL1: betto rodrigues/SS (t), kikujungboy/SS (c), Kobby Dagan/SS (b), **2.1 EL1:** Pagina/SS (l1), rvlsoft/SS (l2), David Evison/SS (r1), Vicky Jirayu/SS (r2), Konstantin L/SS (r3), **2.2 EL1:** Pagina/SS (l1), David Evison/SS (l2), pcruciatti/SS (l3), **3.1 EL1:** Everett Historical/SS (r), **3.2 EL1:** Comaniciu Dan/SS (l1), Gustavo Fadel/SS (l2), Bambax/SS (l3), kikujungboy/SS (l4), **4.1 EL1:** Arena Photo UK/SS (r), **4.2 EL1:** Giovanni G/SS (l1), Martin Hesko/SS (l2), mikecphoto/SS (l3), **5.1 EL1:** Moviestore collection Ltd/Alamy (l), **5.2 EL1:** yurchak/SS (l1), mhatzapa/SS (l2), Marynchenko Oleksandr/SS (c), lineartestpilot/SS (r2), Marynchenko Oleksandr/SS (b), **6.1:** Kobby Dagan/SS (c) **PPT 1:** kikujungboy/SS (1r), betto rodrigues/SS (2l), Pawel Pajor/SS (2r), 3DProfi/SS (3r), **PPT 2:** pcruciatti/SS (1c), pcruciatti/SS (2l), pcruciatti/SS (3c), **PPT 3:** Everett Historical/SS (1c), astudio/SS (2c), Bambax/SS (3l), Comaniciu Dan/SS (3tr), Gustavo Fadel/SS (3br), **PPT 4:** Phil MacD Photography/SS (1c), Giovanni G/SS (2tl), pio3/SS (2tr), mikecphoto/SS (2b), Martin Hesko/SS (3tr), **PPT 5:** © David Holbrook / Alamy Stock Photo (1l), Marynchenko Oleksandr/SS (2b), FOOTBALL (2l), lineartestpilot/SS (2cl), yurchak/SS (2cr), mhatzapa/SS (2r), **PPT 6:** Olga Yatsenko/SS (1c), Pixel Embargo/SS (2r), Picsfive/SS (3c)

Travel

1.1 EL1: mahfud21/SS (l1), Vasilyeva Larisa/SS (l2), mahfud21/SS (l3), AXA/SS (l4), Sign N Symbol Production/SS (l5), Bistraffic/SS (l6), Sign N Symbol Production/SS (c1), Michal Jurkowski/SS (c2), robuart/SS (c3), olegtoka/SS (c4), LANTERIA/SS (c5), Michal Jurkowski/SS (c6), KannaA/SS (r1), KannaA/SS (r2), Vasilyeva Larisa/SS (r3), kotikoti/SS (r4), **1.1a EL2/3:** KannaA/SS (l), mahfud21/SS (r1), Sign N Symbol Production/SS (r2), Vasilyeva Larisa/SS (r3), Michal Jurkowski/SS (r4), **1.2 EL1:** robuart/SS (l1), 09910190/SS (l2), Sentavio/SS (l3), larryrains/SS (l4), mahfud21/SS (l5), gilev stepan/SS (l6), XiXinXing/SS (r), **2.1 EL1:** Michal Jurkowski/SS (l1), faysal/SS (l2), Palto/SS (l3), Vertes Edmond Mihai/SS (l4), TijanaM/SS (r1), Rauf Aliyev/SS (r2), **2.1 EL2:** Palto/SS (l1), Vertes Edmond Mihai/SS (l2), TijanaM/SS (r1), mahfud21/SS (r2), **2.2 EL1:** Vertes Edmond Mihai/SS (r1), Palto/SS (r2), Michal Jurkowski/SS (r3), Rauf Aliyev/SS (r4), TijanaM/SS (r5), mahfud21/SS (r6), faysal/SS (r7), **3.1 EL1:** jesadaphorn/SS (l1), Robert Adrian Hillman/SS (l2), martinlubpl/SS (l3), stockshoppe/SS (r1), Ariadna Ada Sysoeva/SS (r2), Steinar/SS (r3), **3.2 EL1:** Arena Photo UK/SS (l1), Mark William Richardson/SS (l2), Hayati Kayhan/SS (r1), chaoss/SS (r2), **3.2 EL2:** Hayati Kayhan/SS (l1), chaoss/SS (l2), Arena Photo UK/SS (r1), Mark William Richardson/SS (r2), Aleksandar Todorovic/SS (r3), **4.2 EL1:** ColinCramm/SS (tl), Proskurina Yuliya/SS (cl), Yulia Glam/SS (c), VladisChern/SS (cr), BeRad/SS (bl), Makkuro GL/SS (br), **5.1 EL1/2/3:** 3Dsculptor/SS (l1), Andrey Armyagov/SS (l2), mania-room/SS (l3), Pikul Noorod/SS (r1), Claudio Divizia/SS (r2), Nadalina/SS (r3), **5.2 EL1/2:** Eugene Sergeev/SS (l1), 3Dsculptor/SS (l2), Andrey Armyagov/SS (l3), Claudio Divizia/SS (l4), Nadalina/SS (l5), Pikul Noorod/SS (l6), mania-room/SS (l7), **6.2 EL1:** Csaba Deli/SS (r1), Antonio Guillem/SS (r2), VladisChern/SS (r3), **6.3/6.4 EL1/2/3:** Stuart Miles/SS (r1), sasha3538/SS (r2), SVStudio/SS (r3), Billion Photos/SS (bl), akud/SS (br) **PPT 1:** WDG Photo/SS (1l), Pecold/SS (1c), aphotostory/SS (1r), Design JP/SS (2tl), Ksanawo/SS (2tr), aarrows/SS (3b), **PPT 2:** sniegirova mariia/SS (1b), Kaspars Grinvalds/SS (2c), **PPT 3:** Paul Daniels/SS (1bl), Pefkos/SS (1tr), **PPT 4:** Aleksandar Todorovic/SS (1b), EpicStockMedia/SS (2l), liewluck/SS (2r), littleny/SS (2b), suradach/SS (3c), **PPT 5:** diversepixel/SS (1b), michaeljung/SS (1r), diversepixel/SS (2b), michaeljung/SS (2c), ullrich/SS (2l), ullrich/SS (2r), GiDesign/SS (3c), **PPT 6:** OPOLJA/SS (1c), Monkey Business Images/SS (2c)

Volunteering

1.1 EL1/2/3: Anton Gvozdikov/SS (c), **1.2 EL1:** Anton Gvozdikov/SS (t), shockfactor.de/SS (bl), Melica/SS (bc), shockfactor.de/SS (br), **1.2 EL2:** Anton Gvozdikov/SS (t), **2.1/2.2 EL1/2/3:** Ermolaev Alexander/SS (t), **3.1 EL1:** Ivan Ryabokon/SS (l), majivecka/SS (r1), agrino/SS (r2), **3.1 EL2:** Olga1818/SS (t), Ivan Ryabokon/SS (c), Ermolaev Alexander/SS (b), **3.2 EL1:** majivecka/SS (tl), agrino/SS (tc), Olga1818/SS (tr), **4.1a EL1:** Hibrida/SS (b1), Yulia Glam/SS (b2), Mascha Tace/SS (b3), Lorelyn Medina/SS (b4), VOOK (b5), **4.2 EL1/2/3:** Olga1818/SS (t), **5.1/5.2 EL1/2:** wavebreakmedia/SS (c), **6.1/2/3 EL1:** Maquiladora/SS (all), **6.2a EL1:** Monkey Business Images/SS (t1), Dora Zett/SS (t2), giSpate/SS (t3), racorn/SS (b1), Kzenon/SS (b2), W_R_Wolf/SS (b3), Monkey Business Images/SS (b4), **6.2b EL1:** Dmytro Zinkevych/SS (t1), Monkey Business Images/SS (t2), Dragon Images/SS (t3), Monkey Business Images/SS (t4), jdwfoto/SS (t5) **PPT 1:** tiverylucky/SS (1c), Anton Gvozdikov/SS (2r), **PPT 2:** Monkey Business Images/SS (1l), jdwfoto/SS (1r), shockfactor.de/SS (2r), Olga1818/SS (3l), Olga1818/SS (3r), **PPT 3:** racorn/SS (1l), Olga1818/SS (1t), Mascha Tace/SS (1r), Kzenon/SS (1b), kudla/SS (3l), kudla/SS (3r), **PPT 4:** Olga1818/SS (1l), Monkey Business Images/SS (1r), **PPT 5:** wavebreakmedia/SS (1l), Monkey Business Images/SS (l2), Lorelyn Medina/SS (2c), **PPT 6:** 3DProfi/SS (1a), Duettographics/SS (2l), Jaaak/SS (2c), Duettographics/SS (2r), Dragon Images/SS (3t), Monkey Business Images/SS (3b)

© HarperCollins*Publishers* 2016

Adventure

1.1 EL1: Archive Pics/Alamy (l1), Archive Pics/Alamy (l2), Mary Evans/SZ Photo/Scherl (l3), deer boy/SS (r1), Illustrated London News Ltd/Mary Evans (r2), Mary Evans Picture Library (r3), Michael Van Woert, NOAA NESDIS (r4), Naeblys/SS (r5), **1.2 EL1:** The National Library of Norway (l1), **2.1 EL1:** Archive Pics/Alamy (l1), Archive Pics/Alamy (l2), WS Collection/Alamy (r1), **2.2 EL1:** Sashkin/SS (tc), **3.1 EL1/2/3:** Moviestore collection Ltd/Alamy (tr), **3.2 EL3:** Rohit Tandon (cr), **5.1 EL1/2:** Milkovasa/SS (tl), Mut Hardman/SS (tr), Emiliano Rodriguez/SS (cl, b2), ruza74/SS (cr, b1), Vangert/SS (b3), Syda Productions/SS (b4), johavel/SS (b5), Konstantin L/SS (b6), Marcos Mesa Sam Wordley/SS (b7), Makkuro GL/SS (b8), **5.1 EL3:** olgasunnyday/SS (c), **5.2 EL1:** maxbelchenko/SS (b1), Emiliano Rodriguez/SS (b2), attilio pregnolato/SS (b3), Federico Rostagno/SS (b4), Vibrant Image Studio/SS (b5), NADA GIRL/SS (b6), Maximchuk/SS (b7), set/SS (b8), **6.1 EL1:** Photobac/SS (b1), Galyna Andrushko/SS (b2), Maridav/SS (b3), Rohit Tandon (b4), Mut Hardman/SS (b5), Ammit Jack/SS (b6), De Visu/SS (b7), Nina Lishchuk/SS (b8), **PPT 1:** Istimages/SS (1l), deer boy/SS (1r), Sergey Goryachev/SS (2r), Mary Evans/SZ Photo/Scherl (3r), **PPT 2:** Archive Pics/Alamy (1l), Archive Pics/Alamy (1r), NirdalArt/SS (2l), Rusalam Mateeyoh/SS (2r), Illustrated London News Ltd/Mary Evans (3l), Naeblys/SS (3c), Mary Evans Picture Library (3r), **PPT3:** Olga Danylenko/SS (1c), Moviestore collection Ltd/Alamy (2c), Rohit Tandon (3c), **PPT 4:** lassedesignen/SS (1l), S_Class/SS (1t), Nina Lishchuk/SS (1b), Evgenia22/SS (2t), Ye Liew/SS (2b1), benjaminec/SS (2b2), RTimages/SS (2b3), pingebat/SS (2b4), **PPT 5:** Emiliano Rodriguez/SS (1c), olgasunnyday/SS (3c), **PPT 6:** Ammit Jack/SS (1c)

Education

1.1 EL1: Trimitrius/SS (t1), Taina Sohlman/SS (t2), Holly Vegter/SS (t3), Javier Brosch/SS (t4), Inga_Ivanova/SS (t5), Remizov/SS (b1), Yanas/SS (b2), robuart/SS (b3), michaeljung/SS (b4), Sergey Novikov/SS (b5), **1.1 EL2:** Neizu/SS (t1), robuart/SS (t2), owatta/SS (t3), JPC-PROD/SS (t4), HeartBeat/SS (t5), Holly Vegter/SS (b1), saravector/SS (b3), **1.2 EL1:** Alexei-DOST/SS (r1), Aleksandr Bryliaev/SS (r2), Taina Sohlman/SS (r3), Inga_Ivanova/SS (r4), autovector/SS (r5), antoniodiaz/SS (r6), **1.2 EL2:** Olga Pink/SS (tl), Jiang Zhongyan/SS (tc), ChristianChan/SS (tr), Robert Przybysz/SS (bl), Adam68/SS (bc), Yellowj/SS (br), lineartestpilot/SS (t1), Victor Brave/SS (t2), Andrey Makurin/SS (t3), iQoncept/SS (t4), artenot/SS (t5), Hanoi Photography/SS (c1), Ljupco Smokovski/SS (c2), Hurst Photo/SS (c3), KWSPhotography/SS (b1), Photographee.eu/SS (b2), pathdoc/SS (b3), **2.2 EL1:** Hurst Photo/SS (t1), Billion Photos/SS (t2), s_karau/SS (t3), Dragon Images/SS (t4), Christos Georghiou/SS (c1), Andrey Makurin/SS (c2), ser_sh/SS (c3), s_karau/SS (b1), Alvin Cadiz/SS (b2), yaistantine/SS (b3), **3.1 EL1:** lynea/SS (tl), IgorGolovniov/SS (bl), Kuznetsov Alexey/SS (br), **3.1 EL2:** Epitavi/SS (bl), **4.1 EL1:** ori-artiste/SS (t), Gts/SS (c), humphrey/SS (b1), blackboard1965/SS (b2), Zethinova/SS (b3), yoshi-5/SS (b4), yoshi-5/SS (b5), MSSA/SS (b6), Billion Photos/SS (b8), **5.1 EL1/2:** DGLimages/SS (t), wavebreakmedia/SS (b), **5.2 EL1:** wavebreakmedia/SS (t1, b), Phovoir/SS (t2), Billion Photos/SS (t3), DGLimages/SS (c), **6.2 EL1:** Naghiyev/SS (r1), Anton Brand/SS (r2), colonga123456/SS (r3), Maksim M/SS (r4), colonga123456/SS (r5), tynyuk/SS (r6), phloxii/SS (r7), **PPT 1:** Yanas/SS (2tr) NirdalArt/SS (2rc), Jiang Zhongyan/SS (2rb), BlueRingMedia/SS (3l), Evgenia 22/SS (3c), **PPT 2:** ©Collins Education, an imprint of HarperCollins Publishers. Drawn by Iva Sasheva (1c), Andrey Makurin/SS (2b1), ser_sh/SS (2t1), yaistantine/SS (2b2), Blueguy/SS (2t2), Dragon Images/SS (3c), **PPT 3:** Kuznetsov Alexey/SS (1l), notkoo/SS (1r), IgorGolovniov/SS (2rt), MAC1/SS (2rc), Aleks Melnik/SS (2rb), Epitavi/SS (3l), lynea/SS (3r), **PPT 4:** blackboard1965/SS (1c), **PPT 5:** kidstudio852/SS (1l, 1rt, 1rb), POM POM/SS (2l), Ivan Garcia/SS (2r), petrroudny43/SS (3bl), Tiplyashina Evgeniya/SS (3br), **PPT 6:** Dragon Images/SS (1c), wenchiawang/SS (2l)

Fashion

1.1 EL1: Paolo Bona/SS (c1), crystalfoto/SS (c2), Nejron Photo/SS (c3), Aleksander Bartnikowski/SS (c4), **1.1 EL2:** Evgenia B/SS (bc), **1.1 EL3:** Zvonimir Atletic/SS (tr), **2.1 EL1/2/3:** Monkey Business Images/SS (t), pcruciatti/SS (b), **2.2 EL1:** wavebreakmedia/SS (l), singh_lens/SS (c), lorimoebius/SS (r), **3.1 EL1:** ArtWell/SS (r1), Monkey Business Images/SS (r2), Syda Productions/SS (r3), Pressmaster/SS (r4), Red On/SS (r5), **3.2 EL2:** Claudio Divizia/SS (b1), Vectorinka/SS (b2), aunaauna/SS (b3), Reservoir Dots/SS (b4), Blablo101/SS (b5), cvm/SS (b6), ivelly/SS (b7), Incomible/SS (b8), **4.1 EL1/2/3:** alexwhite/SS (t), iDesign/SS (l), Elnur/SS (r1), sianc/SS (r2), Kiselev Andrey Valerevich/SS (r3), **4.2 EL1:** sianc/SS (tl), Kiselev Andrey Valerevich/SS (tc), Elnur/SS (tr), Palto/SS (cl), **4.2 EL2/3:** iDesign/SS (l), **5.1 EL1/2:** ©2011-2016 spidergypsy/http://spidergypsy.deviantart.com/ (c), Everett Historical/SS (c1), AF archive/Alamy (c2), North Wind Picture Archives/Alamy (c3), **5.1 EL2:** Moviestore collection Ltd/Alamy (c3), **5.2 EL1:** MAR007/SS (b1), North Wind Picture Archives/Alamy (b2), Minerva Studio/SS (b3), AF archive/Alamy (b4), Moviestore collection Ltd/Alamy (b5), **6.1 EL1:** Aurora72/SS (t1), Comodo777/SS (t2), Lorelyn Medina/SS (t3), mariarita brunazzi/SS (c1), Pavel K/SS (c2), stickerama/SS (c3), Lorelyn Medina/SS (b1), studiostoks/SS (b2), Lindarks/SS (b3), **6.1 EL2:** lorimoebius/SS (t2), **6.2 EL1/2:** Pavel K/SS (t1), Aurora72/SS (t2), Lorelyn Medina/SS (t3), Lorelyn Medina/SS (t4), **6.2 EL1:** Fun Way Illustration/SS (b1), ladyfortune/SS (b2), Evgenia B/SS (b3), Lorelyn Medina/SS (b4), Pavel K/SS (b5), fxmdusan73/SS (b6), Banana Walking/SS (b7), surawutob/SS (b8), **6.2 EL2:** Sergey Merkulov/SS (b1), Pavel K/SS (b2), ladyfortune/SS (b3), Lorelyn Medina/SS (b4), Kakigori Studio/SS (b5), fxmdusan73/SS (b6), Fun Way Illustration/SS (b7), Shutterstock/SS (b8), **PPT 1:** Gordana Sermek/SS (1c), Nejron Photo/SS (2c), **PPT 2:** Monkey Business Images/SS (1l), Christopher Mansfield/SS (1c), wavebreakmedia/SS (1r), Christopher Mansfield/SS (2l), Billion Photos/SS (2r), **PPT 4:** Everett Collection/SS (1tl), Kuznetsov Alexey/SS (1tr), CREATISTA/SS (1bl), Paolo Bona/SS (1br), HUANG Zheng/SS (2c1), PanicAttack/SS (2c2), Kiselev Andrey Valerevich/SS (2c3), fiii/SS (2c4), **PPT 5:** Moviestore collection Ltd/Alamy (1c), North Wind Picture Archives/Alamy (1c), Ysbrand Cosijn/SS (1r), Florilegius/Alamy (2l), AF archive/Alamy (2r), kidstudio852/SS (3c), **PPT 6:** Zorylee Diaz-Lupitou/SS (1l), Sky Cinema/SS (1r), Dragon Images/SS (2c), wongstock/SS (3tr), Lamai Prasitsuwan/SS (3br)

Sport

1.2 EL1/2: Pagina/SS (tr), photo.ua/SS (cr), Natursports/SS (bl), anekoho/SS (br), **2.1 EL1/2:** Iurii Osadchi/SS (t), Alexey Losevich/SS (c), **2.2 EL1:** Iurii Osadchi/SS (t), Matushchak Anton/SS (c), **2.3 EL1/2/3:** Monkey Business Images/SS (tl), Sabphoto/SS (bl), Axente Vlad/SS (br), **3.1 EL1:** Rivan media/SS (tr), Emmoth/SS (tl), Kochergin/SS (bc), **3.1 EL1/2:** Oleh Dubyna/SS (t), mooinblack/SS (c), Maxisport/SS (b), **3.2 EL1/2:** Zilu8/SS (t), mooinblack/SS (c), Maxisport/SS (b), **4.1 EL1:** mooinblack/SS (t), Nejron Photo/SS (b), **4.1 EL1/2:** Fotokvadrat/SS (b), **5.1 EL1:** Luis Molinero/SS (l1), Eugene Onischenko/SS (l2), Nomad_Soul/SS (l3), Ljupco Smokovski/SS (l4), Ljupco Smokovski/SS (l5), Carlos E. Santa Maria/SS (l6), **6.1 EL1:** WilleeCole Photography/SS (b), **6.2 EL1/2/3:** cherezoff/SS (tl), AlinaMD/SS (tc), Matushchak Anton/SS (tr), izamon/SS (cl), WilleeCole Photography/SS (cr), photolinc/SS (bl), marrishuanna/SS (br), **6.3 EL1/2:** Rob Wilson/SS (t), Photo Works/SS (c), Dziurek/SS (b), **6.4 EL1/2/3:** Natursports/SS (l1), Gines Romero/SS (l2), Zilu8/SS (l3), Matushchak Anton/SS (l4), **PPT 1:** Oleksii Sidorov/SS (1c), Pavel L Photo and Video/SS (2c), **PPT 2:** mangostock/SS (1l), ostill/SS (2l), Viorel Sima/SS (2r), Maxisport/SS (3l), **PPT 3:** kak2s/SS (1r), Krivosheev Vitaly/SS (2l), **PPT 4:** Monkey Business Images/SS (1c), AGIF/SS (2l), Monkey Business Images/SS (2r), **PPT 5:** ©Alan Brown 2014 (1c), Krivosheev Vitaly/SS (3c), **PPT 6:** AlinaMD/SS (1l), Mr Twister/SS (1r), tanatat/SS (2r), Gines Romero/SS (3tl), Natursports/SS (3tr), Matushchak Anton/SS (3bl), Zilu8/SS (3br)

Transport

1.1 EL1/2/3: Robert Lazenby/Alamy (l), northallertonman/SS (c), Zurijeta/SS (r), **2.1 EL1/2:** Rob Wilson/SS (r2), Pagina/SS (r3), **2.1 EL1:** Volvio/SS (r1), Oliver Hoffmann/SS (r4), **2.1 EL2:** Borysevych.com/SS (r1), photo.ua/SS (r4), **2.2 EL1:** David Evison/SS (r3), elenaburn/SS (r5), monotoomono/SS (b1), Sabphoto/SS (b2), Jochen Schoenfeld/SS (b3), Borysevych.com/SS (b4), **3.1 EL1:** Rohit Tandon/SS (t2), Cattallina/SS (t3), josh.tagi/SS (t4), Julien Buckley/Alamy/SS (r), **3.1 EL3:** kak2s/SS (c), **3.2 EL1:** Stefano Garau/SS (r1), VectorLifestylepic/SS (r2), Evgeny Bakharev/SS (r3), Antonio Guillem/SS (r4), VladisChern/SS (r5), **4.1 EL1:** sondem/SS (r1), View Apart/SS (r2), Makushin Alexey/SS (r3), grafixx/SS (r4), **4.1a EL2:** View Apart/SS (r3), **5.1 EL1:** Moving Moment/SS (tl), Viacheslav Lopatin/SS (tr), i4lcocl2/SS (bl), Georgios Kollidas/SS (br), **5.2 EL1:** alexwhite/SS (tl), iDesign/SS (l), Viacheslav Lopatin/SS (tr), TungCheung/SS (tr), Michal Jurkowski/SS (r3), i4lcocl2/SS (r4), **6.2a EL1:** Magic Car Pics/REX (t), Vectorinka/SS (c1), DinoZ/SS (c3), Diego Schtutman/SS (c4), HeartBeat/SS (b1), Istimages/SS (b2), Lisa Werner/SS (b3), LI CHAOSHU/SS (b4), Tom Wang/SS (b5), **6.2b EL2:** ducu59us/SS (t1), michaeljung/SS (t2), Kuznetsov Alexey/SS (t3), Radu Bercan/SS (t4), Piotr Marcinski/SS (t5), **6.2b EL2:** KennyK/SS (tc), Nerthuz/SS (l2), Bjorn Heller/SS (l3), topae/SS (r1), Vereshchagin Dmitry/SS (r2), Taina Sohlman/SS (r3), **GCSE Ready:** ProStockStudio/SS (c), **PPT 1:** UK City Images/Alamy (2l), **PPT 2:** Chris Jenner/SS (1bl), Peter Sterling/SS (1br), **PPT 3:** Dooder/SS (1c), advent/SS (2l1), rzstudio/SS (2l2), Ampon Akearunrung/SS (2l3), hvostik/SS (2r2), Spreadthesignh/SS (2r3), Irina Levitskaya/SS (2r4), Holger Leue/LOOK-foto/Getty (3r), **PPT 4:** nathanmcc/SS (2tl), **PPT 5:** kavalenkau/SS (1tr), StudioPortoSabbia/SS (1bl), **PPT 6:** Alona_S/SS (2tl), BWArt/SS (2bl), Arkela/SS (2tr), Kanok Sulaiman/SS (2br), Costazzurra/SS (4r)

Text extracts in GCSE-Ready Worksheets

Celebrities: Based on *The Daily Telegraph*, 29 Nov 2011, **Education:** *Jane Eyre* © Julie Berry 2016, **Fashion:** *Copycat* © Cathy MacPhail 2014, *Little Women* © 2015 Katie Dale, **Sport:** John Percy, *The Daily Telegraph,* 16 April 2016 © Telegraph Media Group Limited